bibingka
steamed coconut
rice cake

bulaklak
flower

T0152146

puting bino
white wine

pulang bino
red wine

Araw ng mga Puso
Valentine's Day

Isa kaming masayang pamilya!
We are a happy family!

sinturon
belt

mangga
mango

TAGALOG
PICTURE
DICTIONARY

LEARN 1,500 TAGALOG WORDS AND EXPRESSIONS

Jan Tristan Arroyo Gaspi
Sining Maria Rosa Marfori

TUTTLE Publishing

Tokyo | Rutland, Vermont | Singapore

Contents

A Basic Introduction to the Tagalog Language

The Philippines and the History of the Filipino Language

The Philippines is an archipelago composed of 7,107 islands. Because of the country's geography, there are over 300 languages and dialects spoken in the country. Filipino is the National Language of the Republic of the Philippines, but it is more popularly known in the world as Tagalog.

Tagalog is the country's lingua franca. It is one of the languages in the Philippines along with Bikol, Ilocano, Ilonggo (Hiligaynon), Kapampangan, Pangasinan, Cebuano, and Waray (Samar-Leyte). These languages are geographically represented by different regions: Ilocano and Pangasinan in Northern Luzon; Kapampangan in Central Luzon; Bicol in Southern Luzon; Cebuano, Ilonggo, and Waray in Visayas and Mindanao; and finally Tagalog in the densely populated National Capital Region and the Southern Tagalog Region in Luzon.

During the pre-colonial period, the natives used baybayin. In the 1930s, Lope K Santos, a Filipino Tagalog language scholar, developed the abakada, which consists of 15 consonants and 5 vowels.

a, b, k, d, e, g, h, i, l, m, n, ng, o, p, r, s, t, u, w, y
a, ba, ka, da, e, ga, ha, i, la, ma, na, nga, o, pa, ra, sa, ta, u, wa, ya

Because research and experience showed that the Tagalog's 20-letter abakada is inadequate for the writing requirements of a national language, eight letters (C, F, J, Ñ, Q, V, X, and Z) were added to the alphabet in 1987; thus, the birth of a 28-letter alphabet, called the Pinagyamanang Alpabeto (Enriched Alphabet). These new letters represent sounds that are absent in Tagalog but present in the other native languages like Ivatan, Ibanag, Ifugaw, Kiniray-a, Mëranaw, Bilaan, etc. It is also then that "Pilipino" was replaced by "Filipino language."

Foreign Origins of Tagalog Words

The Philippines was colonized by Spain for three centuries, the U.S. for four decades, and Japan during the second World War. During the Pre-Colonial Period, indigenous Filipinos traded with Chinese, Arabs, Malays, and Indians. Through time, with Filipinos having constant contact with foreign traders and their colonizers, Tagalog evolved to the language as we know today. A number of foreign words were adapted to the language, using native pronunciation and spelling according to the Philippine alphabet.

Here are some examples of Tagalog words adapted from foreign languages:

Spanish	Tagalog		
cuarto	kuwarto	(ku-war-to)	*room*
bicicleta	bisikleta	(bi-si-kle-ta)	*bicycle*
guapo	guwapo	(gu-wa-po)	*handsome*
carne	karne	(kar-ne)	*meat*
coche	kotse	(ko-che)	*car*
fiesta	piyesta	(pi-yes-ta)	*feast*
silla	silya	(sil-ya)	*chair*

Japanese	Tagalog		
jankenpon	jack en poy	(jack-en-poy)	*rock, paper, scissors*
karaoke	karaoke	(ka-ra-o-ke)	*singing machine*
dandan	dahan-dahan	(da-han-da-han)	*slowly*

English	Tagalog		
nurse	**nars**	(nars)	*nurse*
teacher	**titser**	(tit-ser)	*teacher*
tricycle	**traysikel**	(tray-si-kel)	*tricycle*
computer	**kompyuter**	(kom-pyu-ter)	*computer*
cake	**keyk**	(keyk)	*cake*
boxing	**boksing**	(bok-sing)	*boxing*
traffic	**trapik**	(tra-pik)	*traffic*
alcohol	**alkohol**	(al-ko-hol)	*alcohol*

Pronunciation Guide

The simple golden rule, "**Kung anong baybay, siyang bigkas**," which translates to, "How you say it is how you spell it". To further emphasize, "**Kung anong bigkas, siyang baybay**," which translates to. "How you spell it is how you say it!" Every letter is pronounced, even when there are two, three, or four consecutive vowels in a word.

Key things to remember:
- The vowels do not have much variation
- Pronounce every letter even if they are repeated
- There are no silent letters

Vowels

a like the *a* in *art, adult, another*
e like the *e* in *elf, end, effort, egg*
i like the *i* in *industry, ink, Illinois*
o like the *o* in *off, order, ostrich*
u like the *u* in *food, rude, tune*

Define the syllables when pronouncing the words. Thus, when there are multiple vowels in a word, the vowels must be pronounced separately and not blended.

paalam (pa-a-lam) *goodbye*
makiusap (ma-ki-u-sap not ma-kiyu-sap) *to request*
umuulan (u-mu-u-lan not u-muu-lan) *raining*
pag-iikot (pag-i-i-kot not pag-ii-kot) *getting around*

Vowel Combinations

ia = ya or **iya**   social (so-syal)   dialogue (da-ya-lo-go)   diaper (da-ya-per)
ie = ye or **iye**   pier (pi-yer)   fiesta (pi-yes-ta)   diet (di-ye-ta)
io = yo or **iyo**   pollution (po-lu-syon)   action (ak-syon)   union (un-yon)
ua = wa or **uwa**   sexual (sek-swal)   spiritual (is-pi-rit-wal)   situation (sit-wa-syon)
ue = we or **uwe**   question (kuwes-tyon)
ui = wi or **uwi**   acquisition (ak-wi-si-syon)   biscuit (bis-kwit)   intuition (in-tu-wi-syon)

Consonants

The Tagalog consonants are **b**, **d**, **k**, **g**, **h**, **l**, **m**, **n**, **ng**, **p**, **r**, **s**, **t**, **w**, **y**

b	like the *b* in *b*ack, *b*all, *b*ag	**ng**	like the *ng* in si*ng*er, lo*ng*, bri*ng*
d	like the *d* in *d*og, *d*ark, *d*own	**p**	like the *p* in *p*eople, *p*ig, *p*artner
k	like the *c* in *c*abbage, *c*at, *c*art	**r**	like the *r* in *r*at, *r*ain, *r*ule
g	like the *g* in *g*ate, *g*un, *g*od	**s**	like the *s* in *s*nake, *s*ail, *s*ong
h	like the *h* in *h*at, *h*ead, *h*ome	**t**	like the *t* in *t*in, *t*all, *t*ime
l	like the *l* in *l*ove, *l*amp, *l*ed	**w**	like the *w* in *w*ag, *w*hale, *w*inner
m	like the *m* in *m*an, *m*ind, *m*at	**y**	like the *y* in *y*acht, *y*am, *y*awn
n	like the *n* in *n*ut, *n*ice, *n*one		

* When pronouncing consonants **p**, **k** and **t** make sure that it is not aspirated, meaning there isn't a puff of air coming out of your mouth.

* **ng** is velar nasal. You may find it difficult to produce this sound at first, especially for words that begin with it.

Practice saying these words that begin with **ng** (Pronounce them like you would for the "ng" in "long ago" or "sing along"):

> **ngayon** (nga-yon) *today*
> **ngiti** (ngi-ti) *smile*
> **ngunit** (ngu-nit) *but*
> **ngipin** (ngi-pin) *tooth*

Practice saying these words that have **ng** at the middle position (Pronounce them like you would for the words "singer" and "hanger" and not like "longer", "stronger" or "finger") :

> **pangalan** (pa-nga-lan not pang-ga-lan) *name*
> **pangako** (pa-nga-ko not pang-ga-ko) *promise*
> **bunga** (bu-nga not bung-ga) *fruit*
> **kalinga** (ka-li-nga not ka-ling-ga) *shelter*
> **pahinga** (pa-hi-nga not pa-hing-ga) *rest*

Practice saying these words that have **ng** at the end of the word:

> **tanong** (ta-nong) *question*
> **tulong** (tu-long) *help*
> **piging** (pi-ging) *feast*
> **ningning** (ning-ning) *brightness*
> **kangkong** (kang-kong) *water spinach*

On the other hand, words with **ng** + **g** at the middle are pronounced like "longer", "stronger" and "finger". Pronounce the velar nasal **ng** then the **g** sound.
> Practice saying these words:

> **linggo** (ling-go) *week*
> **pinggan** (ping-gan) *plate*
> **langgam** (lang-gam) *ant*
> **hanggang** (hang-gang) *until*
> **tanggal** (tang-gal) *remove*

Exception to the rule

You will notice that there are exceptions to the rule "How you spell it, is how you say it" when you encounter these common markers:

mga is pronounced as ma-nga
ng (as a stand alone) is pronounced as (nang)

Ito ang bahay ng pamilya ko. (i-to ang ba-hay nang pa-mil-ya ko)
Kinain ng bata ang tanghalian. (ki-na-in nang ba-ta ang tang-ha-li-an)
Bumili siya ng gamit. (bu-mi-li sha nang ga-mit)

Forming Conversational Sentences

In English, the usual sentence structure is (Subject-Verb-Object also known as S-V-O). In the Filipino language, the predicate or verb comes before the subject. You will have to be accustomed to the inverted way because it is the structure that is used in daily conversation.

The sentence *Maria is playing Tennis* (S-V-O) can be translated to **Si Maria ay naglalaro ng Tennis** (S-V-O) and **Naglalaro si Maria ng Tennis** (V-S-O), but in conversational Tagalog, the latter structure is used.

More examples:

S-V-O	S-V-O (formal)	V-S-O (conversational)
He went to the office. S + V	**Siya** ay **pumunta** sa opisina. S + V	**Pumunta siya** sa opisina. V + S
She ate ice cream. S + V + O	**Siya** ay **kumain** ng sorbetes. S + V + O	**Kumain siya** ng sorbetes. V + S + O
Jose will go to the dentist. S + V + O	**Si Jose** ay **pupunta** sa dentista. S + V + O	**Pupunta si Jose** sa dentista. V + S + O

Multiple Meanings

Some words have multiple meanings depending on how the word is pronounced. Changing the position of the stress in a word will change its definition.

Here are some examples:

píto (*whistle*) vs. **pitó** (*seven*)
púno (*tree*) vs. **punó** (*full*)
bása (*read*) vs. **basá** (*wet*)
búhay (*life*) vs. **buháy** (*alive*)

More words and pictures are listed in Chapter 22.

Ways on how to familiarize oneself specifically with verbs and forming sentences on a daily basis

It can be a daunting task to learn what and when to use an affix in a verb. When learning a language it is imperative to say the words, phrases, and most importantly the sentences for memory retention and to become comfortable in sentence construction.

Constructing and saying a sentence at the very moment when you are recalling, doing, and planning about an action is a great way to remember the right usage of an affix in a verb. This would be greatly useful for verbs that are used daily such as: to wake up, to eat, to drink, to leave, to walk, to read, to write, to arrive, to take a shower, to sleep.

Let us take "to eat" as an example. While eating your lunch, construct and say, **"Kumakain ako ng isda."**

(ku-ma-ka-in a-ko nang is-da), "I am eating fish". Follow this with a recollection of what you ate for breakfast, "**Kumain ako ng itlog**" (ku-ma-in a-ko nang it-log), "I ate egg". Finally, start planning on what to eat for dinner by constructing and saying, "**Kakain ako ng spaghetti**" (ka-ka-in a-ko nang spaghetti), "I will eat spaghetti". You just learned the past, present, and future form of the infinitive "**kain**" (ka-in), "to eat". Try doing this routine with the other 9 verbs mentioned for a week until it becomes second-nature.

Once you have mastered the basic structure of Verb + Subject + Object, you can start making your sentences more complex by adding time.

"**Kumakain ako ng isda ngayon**" (ku-ma-ka-in a-ko nang is-da nga-yon)
"I am eating fish right now."

"**Kumain ako ng itlog kaninang umaga**" (ku-ma-in a-ko nang it-log ka-ni-nang u-ma-ga)
" I ate egg earlier this morning."

"**Kakain ako ng spaghetti mamayang gabi**" (ka-ka-in a-ko nang spaghetti ma-ma-yang ga-bi)
"I will eat spaghetti tonight."

This is just one way to learn the Tagalog verbs. Once you get into a habit of this routine, you will be surprised how much words you have learned and how good you have become in constructing sentences within a week.

Here are some of the verbs that are commonly used:

-UM-	IMPERATIVE INFINITIVE	Completed	Incompleted	Contemplated
kain (ka-in) *eat*	**kumain** (ku-ma-in) *to eat*	**kumain** (ku-ma-in) *ate*	**kumakain** (ku-ma-ka-in) *eat/eating*	**kakain** (ka-ka-in) *will eat*
punta (pun-ta) *go*	**pumunta** (pu-mun-ta) *to go*	**pumunta** (pu-mun-ta) *went*	**pumupunta** (pu-mu-pun-ta) *go/going*	**pupunta** (pu-pun-ta) *will eat*
bili (bi-li) *buy*	**bumili** (bu-mi-li) *to buy*	**bumili** (bu-mi-li) *bought*	**bumibili** (bu-mi-bi-li) *buy/buying*	**bibili** (bi-bi-li) *will buy*
gising (gi-sing) *wake up*	gumising (gu-mi-sing) *to wake up*	gumising (gu-mi-sing) *woke up*	gumigising (gu-mi-gi-sing) *wake up/waking up*	gigising (gi-gi-sing) *will wake up*
sakay (sa-kay) *ride*	sumakay (su-ma-kay) *to ride*	sumakay (su-ma-kay) *rode*	sumasakay (su-ma-sa-kay) *ride/riding*	sasakay (sa-sa-kay) *will ride*
baba (ba-ba) *go down*	**bumaba** (bu-ma-ba) *to go down*	**bumaba** (bu-ma-ba) *went down*	**bumababa** (bu-ma-ba-ba) *go down/going down*	**bababa** (ba-ba-ba) *will go down*
takbo (tak-bo) *run*	**tumakbo** (tu-mak-bo) *to run*	**tumakbo** (tu-mak-bo) *ran*	**tumatakbo** (tu-ma-tak-bo) *run/running*	**tatakbo** (ta-tak-bo) *will run*
alis (a-lis) *leave*	**umalis** (u-ma-lis) *to leave*	**umalis** (u-ma-lis) *left*	**umaalis** (u-ma-a-lis) *leave/leaving*	**aalis** (a-a-lis) *will leave*

-UM-	IMPERATIVE INFINITIVE	Completed	Incompleted	Contemplated
uwi (u-wi) *go home*	umuwi (u-mu-wi) *to go home*	umuwi (u-mu-wi) *went home*	umuuwi (u-mu-u-wi) *go home/going home*	uuwi (u-u-wi) *will go home*
inom (i-nom) *drink*	uminom (u-mi-nom) *to drink*	uminom (u-mi-nom) *drank*	umiinom (u-mi-i-nom) *drink/drinking*	iinom (i-i-nom) *will drink*
akyat (ak-yat) *go up*	umakyat (u-mak-yat) *to go up*	umakyat (u-mak-yat) *went up*	umaakyat (u-ma-ak-yat) *go up/going up*	aakyat (a-ak-yat) *went up*

MAG-	IMPERATIVE INFINITIVE	Completed	Incompleted	Contemplated
bayad (ba-yad) *pay*	magbayad (mag-ba-yad) *to pay*	nagbayad (nag-ba-yad) *paid*	nagbabayad (nag-ba-ba-yad) *pay/paying*	magbabayad (mag-ba-ba-yad) *will pay*
kita (ki-ta) *meet up*	magkita (mag-ki-ta) *to meet up*	nagkita (nag-ki-ta) *met up*	nagkikita (nag-ki-ki-ta) *meet up/meeting up*	magkikita (mag-ki-ki-ta) *will meet up*
sundo (sun-do) *pick up*	magsundo (mag-sun-do) *to pick up*	nagsundo (nag-sun-do) *picked up*	nagsusundo (nag-su-sun-do) *pick up/picking up*	magsusundo (mag-su-sun-do) *will pick up*
lakad (la-kad) *walk*	maglakad (mag-la-kad) *to walk*	naglakad (nag-la-kad) *walked*	naglalakad (nag-la-la-kad) *walk/walking*	maglalakad (mag-la-la-kad) *will walk*
pahinga (pa-hi-nga) *rest*	magpahinga (mag-pa-hi-nga) *to rest*	nagpahinga (nag-pa-hi-nga) *rested*	nagpapahinga (nag-pa-pa-hi-nga) *rest/resting*	magpapahinga (mag-pa-pa-hi-nga) *will rest*

Using this Picture Dictionary

Visual learning is essential in learning a foreign language since one can remember a word through visual representation. This book juxtaposes pictures of the words to enable visual learning. Each chapter has a set of words pertaining to the topic of that chapter. There are phrases at the end of each chapter that are examples on how one can use the words listed in a sentence. Do not limit yourself with the words on one chapter when constructing a sentence. As you go through the chapters, start combining words and construct sentences using the V+S+O format. Furthermore, use the verbs listed above to construct sentences using different tenses.

With regard to the audio recordings, choose a topic the best interests you and familiarize yourself with the words while playing the audio recordings. Note the correct pronunciation of the words and mimic them. This will help you memorize the vocabulary and short phrases in each topic.

Having a wide vocabulary will surely help in proceeding to forming sentences if you decide to advance in speaking Tagalog. You can always refer to our other books, *Instant Tagalog* and *Essential Tagalog* for more useful phrases and sentences that you can use in everyday conversation.

1 | Ikinagagalak kong Makilala ka!
So Nice to See You!

1 Hello, kumusta ka?
Hello, how are you?

8 ano?
what?

9 kontento
satisfied

2 Mabuti, salamat!
I am fine, thank you!

3 makilala (to be acquainted);
makipagkilala (to get to know);
makipagkita (to meet in person)
to meet

4 Pedro, siya si Maria.
Pedro, this is Maria.

10 masaya
happy

11 masayahin
joyful

5 Hello!
Hello!

6 Ikinagagalak kong makilala ka!
Pleased to meet you!

7 ipakilala
to introduce

12 tawagan (to call
on the phone);
tawagin to call;
to be called

13 mga kaibigan
friends

15 Hi, Juan ang pangalan ko. Anong pangalan mo?
Hi, my name is Juan. What's your name?

16 Reyes ang apelyido ko, Maria ang unang pangalan ko. Heto ang I.D. ko.
My surname is Reyes, first name Maria. Here's my namecard.

14 ipakilala ang sarili
introduce yourself

Additional Vocabulary

23 pangalan
name

24 apelyido
surname

25 kayo
you (polite)

26 alamin; malaman
to know

27 nasyonalidad
nationality

28 magkamayan
shake hands

29 yumakap; yakapin
to hug

30 humalik; halikan
to kiss

31 ngiti
smile

32 kumaway
to wave

33 yumuko
to bow

34 bumati
to greet

35 magsimula ng usapan
to start a conversation

36 makipagkuwentuhan
to make small talk

37 makipag-usap; makipagtsismisan
to chat; to gossip

38 Kumusta ang mga bagay-bagay?
How are things?

39 Bakit?
Why?

40 iparating (ang pag-bati)
to express (good wishes)

41 barkada
group of friends

17 Paalam! Hanggang sa muli!
Goodbye! See you!

18 Ingat!
Take care!

21 Salamat
Thank you!

22 Wala iyon!
Not at all!

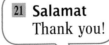

19 pagtitipon; pulong
gathering; meeting

20 pagtitipon; pulong
bisita; kostomer; suki
guest; customer; frequent customer

2 | (Ang) Aking Pamilya
My Family

1 anak na lalake
son

2 lalaki
male

3 babae
female

5 mga bata
children

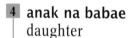

4 anak na babae
daughter

6 mga magulang
parents

Additional Vocabulary

26 asawa
wife

27 asawa
husband

28 nakababatang kapatid na lalaki ng tatay; tito
father's younger brother

29 kapatid na babae ng tatay; tita
father's sister

30 kapatid na lalaki ng nanay; tito
mother's brother

31 manugang
son/daughter-in-law

32 balae
parents of son/daughter-in law

33 lalaking apo; babaeng apo
grandson; granddaughter

34 mga kamag–anak
relatives

35 kapitbahay
neighbor

36 bayaw
brother-in-law

37 hipag
sister-in-law

38 ninong
godfather

39 ninang
godmother

40 pamilya
family

41 sarili
self

42 bata
young

43 masigasig
enthusiastic

44 maniwala
to believe

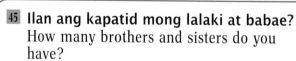

45 Ilan ang kapatid mong lalaki at babae?
How many brothers and sisters do you have?

46 May isa akong ate at isang nakababatang kapatid na lalaki.
I have one elder sister and one younger brother.

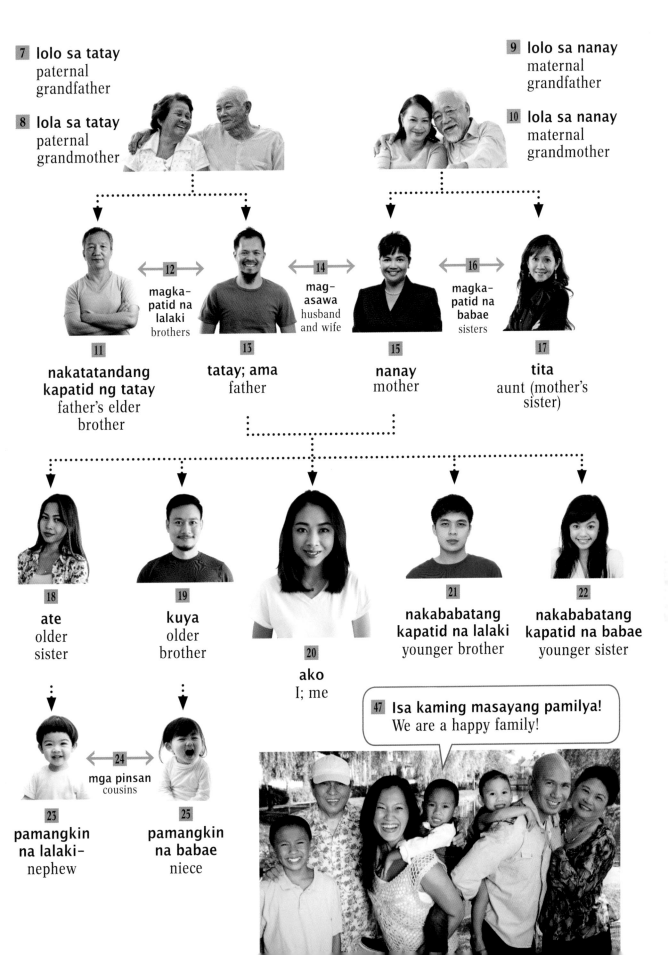

3 Ang Aking Bahay
My House

1 sala
living room

2 balkonahe
balcony

3 rehas
railing

4 kisame
ceiling

5 mga susi
keys

6 larawan; likhang-sining
painting

7 lampara
lamp

8 upuan
chair

9 dingding
wall

10 telebisyon
television

11 mesa para sa kape
coffee table

12 karpet; alpombra
carpet

13 erkon
air conditioner

14 lamesa
table

15 sopa
sofa

16 sahig
floor

17 kurtina
curtain

18 bintana
window

19 unan
pillow

20 kama
bed

21 kuwarto; silid-tulugan
bedroom

22 kuwarto
room

Additional Vocabulary

49 swits ng ilaw
light switch

50 saksakan
electric socket; power point

51 apartment; bahay
apartment; house

52 paupahan
apartment

53 bubong
roof

54 silid sa itaas ng bahay; kuwarto sa itaas ng bahay
attic; loft

55 silid sa ibaba ng bahay; kuwarto sa ibaba ng bahay; silong
basement; cellar

56 garahe
garage

57 Napakagandang bahay! Gusto kong tumira dito!
What a beautiful house! I would love to live here!

14

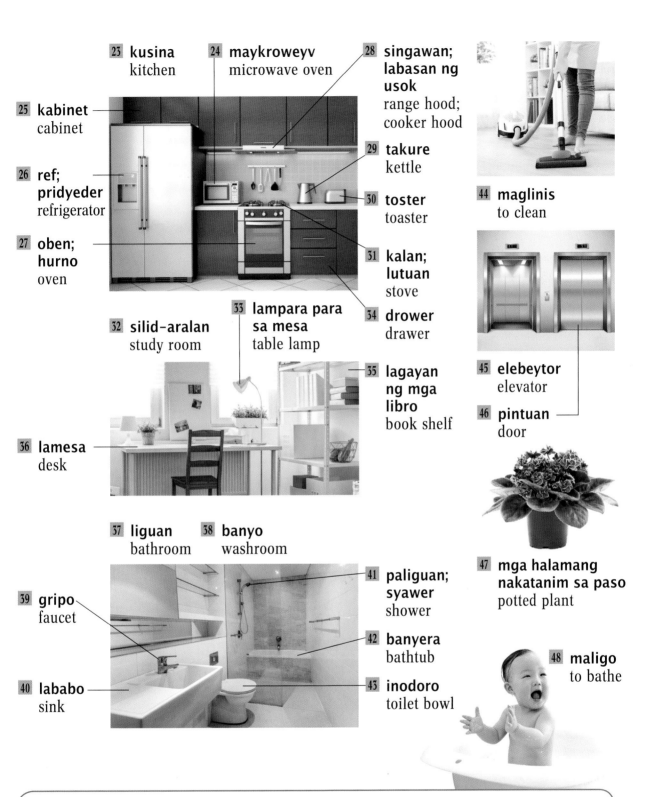

23 **kusina**
kitchen

24 **maykroweyv**
microwave oven

28 **singawan; labasan ng usok**
range hood; cooker hood

25 **kabinet**
cabinet

29 **takure**
kettle

26 **ref; pridyeder**
refrigerator

30 **toster**
toaster

44 **maglinis**
to clean

27 **oben; hurno**
oven

31 **kalan; lutuan**
stove

33 **lampara para sa mesa**
table lamp

32 **silid-aralan**
study room

34 **drower**
drawer

35 **lagayan ng mga libro**
book shelf

45 **elebeytor**
elevator

46 **pintuan**
door

36 **lamesa**
desk

37 **liguan**
bathroom

38 **banyo**
washroom

47 **mga halamang nakatanim sa paso**
potted plant

41 **paliguan; syawer**
shower

39 **gripo**
faucet

42 **banyera**
bathtub

48 **maligo**
to bathe

40 **lababo**
sink

43 **inodoro**
toilet bowl

---

58 **Ilang palapag mayroon ang bahay na ito?**
How many floors does this house have?

60 **Napakalaking bahay!**
What a big house!

59 **Gusto kong umupa ng isang apartment.**
I would like to rent an apartment.

61 **Gusto kong makita ang kusina.**
I want to see the kitchen.

15

4 | (Ang) Katawan ng Tao
The Human Body

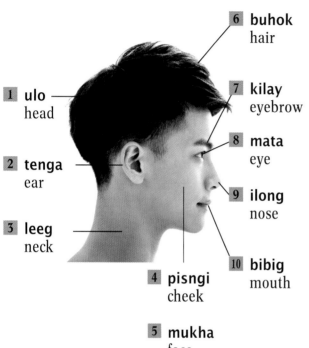

1 ulo
head

2 tenga
ear

3 leeg
neck

6 buhok
hair

7 kilay
eyebrow

8 mata
eye

9 ilong
nose

10 bibig
mouth

4 pisngi
cheek

5 mukha
face

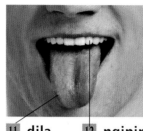

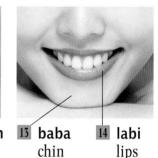

11 dila
tongue

12 ngipin
teeth

13 baba
chin

14 labi
lips

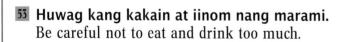

15 mga daliri
fingers

16 mga daliri sa paa
toes

---

50 Ilang bahagi ng katawan ang kaya mong pangalanan?
How many parts of your body can you name?

51 Paano mo inaalagaan ang katawan mo?
How do you take care of your body?

52 Masama sa kalusugan mo ang paninigarilyo.
Smoking is bad for your health.

53 Huwag kang kakain at iinom nang marami.
Be careful not to eat and drink too much.

54 Huwag kang kumain nang masyadong maraming matatamis at tsitsiriya.
Don't eat too many sweets and snacks.

55 Upang manatiling malusog, dapat kang mag-ehersisyo araw-araw.
To stay healthy, you should exercise every day.

17 noo
forehead

24 balikat
shoulder

25 masel
muscles

18 kamay
hand

26 dibdib
chest

27 tiyan
abdomen

19 braso
arm

20 siko
elbow

28 hita
thigh

21 tuhod
knee

22 binti
leg

29 bukung-
bukong
ankle

23 paa
foot

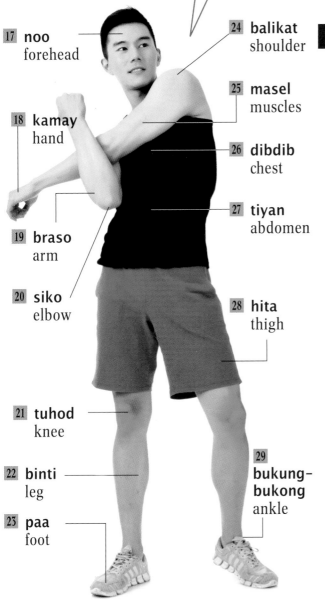

Additional Vocabulary

36 lamang loob
organs

37 sistemang
dihestibo
digestive system

38 sistemang
respiratoryo
respiratory system

39 sistemang
nerbyo
nervous system

40 sistemang
skeletal
skeletal system

41 balat
skin

42 dugo
blood

43 daluyan ng
dugo
vessels

44 buto
bone

45 arterya
artery

46 ugat
vein

47 kalusugan
health

48 sakit; karam-
daman
illness

49 tiyan
stomach

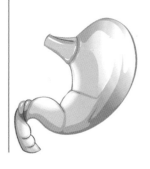

30 utak
brain

31 baga
lungs

32 puso
heart

33 bato
kidneys

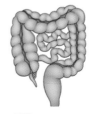
34 bituka
intestines

35 atay
liver

5 | Pagbibilang at mga Numero
Counting and Numbers

1 isa
one

2 dalawa
two

3 tatlo
three

4 apat
four

5 lima
five

6 anim
six

7 pito
seven

8 walo
eight

9 siyam
nine

10 sampu
ten

12 tatlong kapat
three quarters

14 isang katlo
one third

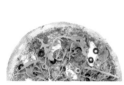
11 kalahati
one half

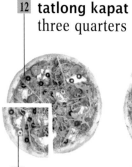

13 isang-kapat
one quarter

15 dalawang katlo
two thirds

Cardinal Numbers
Numerong Kardinal

0 **sero** zero
11 **labing-isa** eleven
12 **labindalawa** twelve
13 **labintatlo** thirteen
14 **labing-apat** fourteen
15 **labinlima** fifteen
16 **labing-anim** sixteen
17 **labimpito** seventeen
18 **labingwalo** eighteen
19 **labinsiyam** nineteen
20 **dalawampu** twenty
21 **dalawampu't isa** twenty-one
22 **dalawampu't dalawa**
   twenty-two
23 **dalawampu't tatlo** twenty-three
24 **dalawampu't apat** twenty-four
25 **dalawampu't lima** twenty-five
26 **dalawampu't anim** twenty-six
27 **dalawampu't pito** twenty-seven
28 **dalawampu't walo** twenty-eight
29 **dalawampu't siyam** twenty-nine
30 **tatlumpu** thirty
40 **apatnapu** forty
50 **limampu** fifty
60 **animnapu** sixty
70 **pitompu** seventy
80 **walumpu** eighty
90 **siyamnapu** ninety
100 **isang daan** one hundred
1,000 **isang libo** one thousand
10,000 **sampung libo** ten thousand
100,000 **isang daang libo**
   one hundred thousand
1,000,000 **isang milyon** one million
100,000,000 **isang daang milyon**
   one hundred million
1,000,000,000 **isang bilyon**
   one billion
10,000,000,000 **sampung bilyon**
   ten billion

16 kalkyuleytor
calculator

17 hatiin
to divide

18 paramihin
to multiply

19 bawasan
to subtract

20 dagdagan
to add

**21 sumatotal;
kalalabasan**
equals

Ordinal Numbers **Numerong Ordinal**

1st **una** first
2nd **pangalawa/ikalawa** second
3rd **pangatlo/ikatlo** third
4th **pang-apat/ika-apat** fourth
5th **panlima/ikalima** fifth
6th **pang-anim/ika-anim** sixth
7th **pampito/ikapito** seventh
8th **pangwalo/ikawalo** eighth
9th **pansiyam/ikasiyam** ninth
10th **pansampu/ikasampu** tenth
11th **panlabing-isa/ikalabing-isa** eleventh
12th **panlabindalawa/ikalabindalawa** twelfth
13th **panlabintatlo/ikalabintatlo** thirteenth
20th **pandalawampu/ikadalawampu** twentieth
30th **pantatlumpu/ikatatlumpu** thirtieth
40th **pang-apatnapu/ika-apatnapu** fourtieth
50th **panlimampu/ikalimampu** fiftieth
60th **pang-animnapu/ika-animnapu** sixtieth
70th **pampitumpu/ikapitumpu** seventieth
80th **pangwalompu/ikawalompu** eightieth
90th **pansiyamnapu/ikasiyamnapu** ninetieth
100th **pang-isandaan/ika-isandaan**
  one-hundredth
1,000th **pang-isanlibo/ika-isanlibo**
  one-thousandth

Additional Vocabulary

22 pareho
two; both

23 porsiyento
percent (%)

**24 maliit na
bahagi;
praksyon**
fraction

25 numerong even
even numbers

26 numerong odd
odd numbers

27 magbilang
to count

28 mga numero
numbers

29 mga numero
digits

**30 Dalawa dagdagan ng apat
ay anim.**
Two plus four equals six.

**31 Labing-isa bawasan ng
lima ay anim**
Eleven minus five equals six.

**32 Sampu paramihin nang labindalawang beses ay
isang daan at dalawampu**
Ten times twelve equals one hundred and twenty.

**33 Apatnapu't dalawa hatiin sa walo ay lima at
sangkapat**
Forty-two divided by eight equals five and a quarter.

19

6 | Pang-araw-araw na Aktibidad
Daily Activities

1 makinig
to listen

2 tingnan; makita
to look; see

5 tumayo
to stand

6 umupo
to sit

3 umiyak
to cry

4 tumawa
to laugh

Additional Vocabulary

18 tunog
sound

19 magtanong
to ask

20 maglaro
to play

21 huminga
to breathe

22 sumagot
to answer

23 makita
to catch sight of

24 magtrabaho; matapos sa trabaho
go to work; get off work

25 pumunta sa paaralan
go to school

26 wala nang pasok
school is over

27 magluto; maghanda ng makakain
to cook; to prepare a meal

28 mag-syawer
to have a shower

29 hugasan ang buhok ko
to wash my hair

30 magpahinga; magrelaks
to relax

31 mag-almusal
to have breakfast

32 mananghalian
to have lunch

33 maghapunan
to have dinner

34 libangan
leisure

35 oras ng pag-aaral
study time

36 gumawa ng gawaing-bahay
to do household chores

37 karaniwang araw
weekday

38 katapusan ng linggo
weekend

39 magalit
to get angry

40 maresolba
to resolve

41 makiusap
to request

42 magkusa
to be willing (to do something)

43 sumang-ayon
to agree

44 Kailangan ko ng walong oras na tulog araw-araw.
I need eight hours of sleep every day.

8 manood ng TV
to watch TV

9 magsulat
to write

7 matulog
to sleep

10 gumising
to wake up

11 magsipilyo
to brush teeth

12 mag-usap
to talk

13 magsalita
to speak

15 maglipat
to move

16 tumulong
to help

17 ilakad ang aso
to walk the dog

14 Magkakasabay kumain ang lahat.
Everybody eats together.

45 Anong ginagawa mo tuwing gabi ng mga araw na may pasok/karaniwang araw?
What do you do on weekday evenings?

46 Ano ang ginagawa mo tuwing katapusan ng linggo?
What do you do on weekends?

47 Ano ang una mong ginagawa tuwing umaga?
What is the first thing you do every morning?

48 Naliligo ako at nagsisipilyo.
I take a shower and brush my teeth.

7 | Mga Kulay, Hugis at Laki
Colors, Shapes and Sizes

1 **mga kulay**
colors

2 **pula**
red

3 **puti**
white

4 **itim**
black

5 **dilaw**
yellow

6 **asul**
blue

7 **berde**
green

8 **ube**
purple

9 **kulay tsokolate**
brown

10 **abo**
gray

11 **kahel**
orange

12 **rosas**
pink

13 **ginto**
gold

14 **pilak**
silver

15 **madilim na kulay**
dark color

16 **maliwanag na kulay**
light color

44 **Ano ang paborito mong kulay?**
What is your favorite color?

45 **Pula ang paborito kong kulay.**
My favorite color is red.

17 **bahaghari**
a rainbow

18 **parihaba**
a rectangle

19 **bilog**
a circle

20 **oktagon; walu-hang-sulok**
an octagon

21 **pentagon; lima-hang-sulok**
a pentagon

22 **parisukat**
a square

23 **puso**
a heart

24 **obalo; hugis-itlog**
an oval

25 **bituin**
a star

26 **tatsulok**
a triangle

27 **heksagon; animang-sulok**
a hexagon

28 **dyamante**
a diamond

29 **laki ng kasuotan**
clothing size

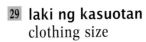

31 **maliit na sukat**
S size

32 **sobrang liit na sukat**
XS size

35 **malaki**
large

36 **katamtaman**
medium

37 **maliit**
small

30 **katamta-mang sukat**
M size

33 **malaking sukat**
L size

34 **sobrang laking sukat**
XL size

42 **May mas malaking sukat ba kayo?**
Do you have a larger size?

Additional Vocabulary

38 **hugis**
shape

39 **sukat**
size

40 **mas malaki**
larger

41 **mas maliit**
smaller

43 **May ibang kulay ba kayo nito?**
Do you have this in other colors?

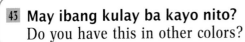

23

8 Magkasalungat
Opposites

1 taas ↔ baba
up   down

2 tanggap ↔ bigay
receive   give

3 mas marami ↔ mas kaunti
more   less

6 labasan ↔ pasukan
exit   enter

4 luma ↔ bago
old   new

5 matangkad ↔ pandak
tall   short

7 mabuti ↔ masama
good   bad

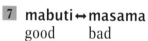

8 abala ↔ walang ginagawa
busy   idle

9 mahaba ↔ maikli
long   short

10 matanda ↔ bata
old   young

11 malaki ↔ maliit
big   small

12 bukas ↔ sarado
open   closed

13 mataba ↔ payat
fat   skinny

32 **Malungkot ang kabaliktaran ng masaya.**
The opposite of happy is sad.

33 **Isang pares din na magkasalungat ang malamig at mainit.**
Cold and hot is also a pair of opposites.

34 **Isang pares ng mga salita na may magkasalungat na kahulugan ang antonim.**
An antonym is a pair of words with opposite meanings.

14 **isuot ↔ hubarin**
put on   take off

15 **mahirap ↔ madali**
difficult   easy

16 **mayroon ↔ wala**
have   do not have

17 **pumunta ↔ umalis**
come   go

18 **oo ↔ hindi**
yes   no

19 **busog ↔ gutom**
full   hungry

20 **dumating ↔ umalis**
arrive   depart

21 **sa loob ↔ sa labas**
inside   outside

22 **nakaraan ↔ hinaharap**
past   future

23 **simula ↔ katapusan**
begin   end

24 **malapit ↔ malayo**
near   far

25 **mali ↔ tama**
wrong   right

26 **tunay ↔ peke**
real   fake

27 **mabilis ↔ mabagal**
fast   slow

28 **mataas ↔ mababa**
high   low

29 **hiramin ↔ ibalik**
borrow   return

30 **nakalimutan ↔ naalala**
forgotten   remembered

31 **malungkot ↔ masaya**
sad   happy

9 Usapang Pera
Money Talk

1 Pesos—opisyal na pera ng Pilipinas.
Pesos–the official currency of the Philippines.

2 barya
coins

3 sentimo
cent

4 dalawampu't limang sentimo
25 cents

5 sampung sentimo
10 cents

6 limang sentimo
5 cents

7 isang sentimo
1 cent

8 papel na pera; buong pera
paper currency

9 dolyar
dollar

10 piso
peso

11 isang piso; piso
1 peso

12 limang piso
5 pesos

13 sampung piso
10 pesos

14 dalawampung piso
20 pesos

15 limampung piso
50 pesos

16 isang daang piso
100 pesos

17 limandaang piso
500 pesos

18 isanlibong piso
1000 pesos

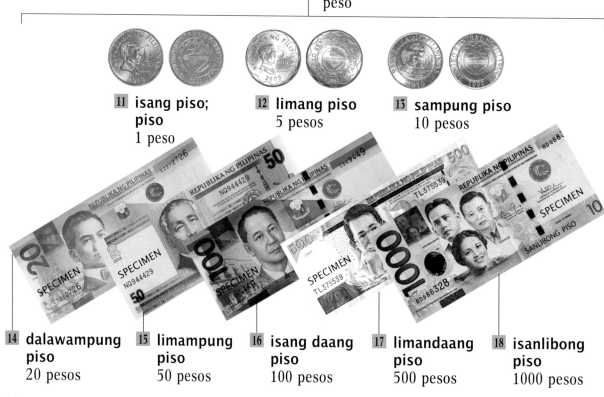

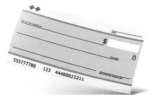

19 tseke
check

20 barya
small change

21 kredit kard
credit card

22 ipon
savings

23 palitan ng pera
currency exchange

24 maglabas ng pera
to withdraw money

25 pera
money

26 presyo
price

27 diskuwento
discount

28 mura
cheap

29 mahal
expensive

30 tubo
interest

31 utang; kredit
loan; credit

32 utang
debt

33 deposito sa bangko
bank deposit

34 numero ng akawnt
account number

35 resibo
receipt

36 hulugang bayad
installment (payment)

37 buwis
tax

38 cash
cash

39 Limampung piso ang palitan ngayon sa isang dolyar.
The current exchange rate for a dollar is 50 Pesos.

40 Puwede ba akong tumawad?
Can I haggle (the price)?

41 Magkano ito?
How much does this cost?

42 Tatlong daang piso.
Three hundred pesos (PHP300).

43 Puwede mo ba akong bigyan ng diskuwento?
Can you give a discount?

44 Sige, sampung porsyentong diskuwento.
OK, 10% discount.

10 | Pamimili
Going Shopping

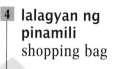

4 **lalagyan ng pinamili**
shopping bag

1 **bumili**
to buy

43 **Magkano?**
How much is it?

2 **magbenta**
to sell

3 **mamili**
to shop

5 **relo**
watch

6 **mga damit**
clothes

11 **salamin**
glasses; spectacles

14 **polo**
shirt

7 **blusa**
blouse

12 **medyas**
socks

15 **kurbata**
necktie

9 **pantalon**
jeans

10 **damit pambaba**
trousers

13 **sapatos**
shoes

16 **sombrero**
hat

8 **palda**
skirt

Some useful shopping expressions:

46 Nasaan ang pinakamalapit na shopping center?
Where is the nearest shopping center?

47 Maaari ko bang subukan ito?
Can I try it on?

48 Nasaan ang silid-sukatan?
Where is the fitting room?

49 Masyadong mahal!
That's too expensive!

50 Kukunin ko ito.
I'll take it.

51 Tumatanggap ba kayo ng kredit kards?
Do you accept credit cards?

52 Magbabayad ako ng cash.
I'll pay in cash.

53 Maaari ba akong magkaroon ng resibo?
Could I have a receipt?

Additional Vocabulary

21 tiangge
bazaar

22 tindahan
shop

23 tindahan sa mall
department store

24 maliit na tindahan
boutique

25 tindera sa tindahan
shop staff

26 kahera
cashier

27 hatid sa bahay
home delivery

28 pagkukumpara ng presyo
comparing prices

29 pamimili sa internet
online shopping

30 kredit kard
credit card

31 kapareho ng
the same as

32 lahat
altogether

33 walang duda
certainly

34 sa pangkalahatan
generally

35 mas marami
more; even more

36 desisyon; pasiya
decision

37 iba
other

38 magdala
to bring

39 mga gamit
things

40 bil; kuwenta
bill; invoice

41 walang buwis
tax free

42 pagsauli sa ibinayad
refund

17 pampaganda
cosmetics

18 mga laruan
toys

19 sinturon
belt

20 bandana
scarf

44 May kasama ba itong buwis?
Is there any tax on this?

45 Puwede ko bang ipasauli ang ibinayad na buwis mamaya?
Can I refund the tax later?

11 Buhay sa Lungsod
Life in the City

1 otel
hotel

2 paliparan; erport
airport

3 tindahan **4 kalye**
shop   street

5 groseri
supermarket

6 istasyon ng gas
gas station;
petrol station

7 bangko
bank

8 lugar ng kumpe-rensiya
conference center

9 istasyon ng tren
train station

10 museo
museum

11 lungsod; siyudad
city

12 napakataas na gusali
skyscraper

13 apartment
apartment building

14 museong pansining
art museum

15 istadyum
stadium

16 pos opis
post office

17 pamilihan; mall
shopping center;
mall

18 ekspreswey
expressway

19 dyim
gym

Additional Vocabulary

20 sinehan
cinema

21 istasyon ng pulis
police station

22 bayan; sentro
downtown

23 sentral na distrito ng negosyo
central business district (CBD)

24 labas ng lungsod
suburb

25 apartment; bahay
apartment;
house

26 tulay
bridge

27 bangketa
sidewalk

28 ilaw pantrapiko
traffic lights

29 kalye
road

30 kapitbahay
neighbor

31 kanto
street corner

32 monumento
monument

33 simbahan
church

34 trapiko
traffic

35 pedestriyan
pedestrian

36 tawiran ng mga pedestriyan
pedestrian
crossing

37 templo
temple

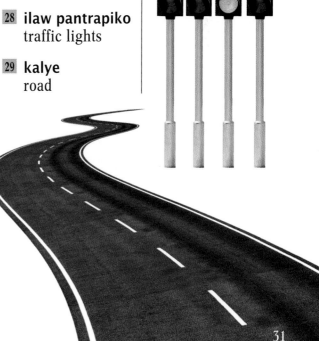

38 Nakatira ka ba sa lungsod? O sa labas ng lungsod?
Do you live in the city? Or in the suburbs?

39 Paano ka pumupunta sa trabaho?
How do you go to work?

40 Gaano kalayo ang paliparan mula sa sentro ng lungsod?
How far is the airport from the city center?

41 Gustong tumira ni Miss Reyes sa lungsod
Miss Reyes wants to live in the city.

31

12 | Paglilibot
Getting Around

1 kotse
car

2 taksi
taxi

3 drayber
driver

4 eroplano
airplane

5 trak
truck

6 trak ng basura
garbage truck

7 tagahatid na van
delivery van

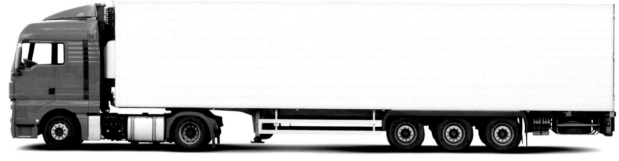

8 mabilis na tren
high speed train

9 motorsiklo;
motor
motorcycle

10 kotseng pang-
isports
sports car

13 **sakayan ng bus**
bus stop

11 **daan sa ilalim ng lupa**
subway

12 **pampublikong bus**
public bus

14 **barko; bangka**
ship; boat

15 **tren**
train

16 **pamatay-sunog na trak**
fire engine

17 **traysikel**
tricycle

18 **dyip**
jeepney

Additional Vocabulary

19 **bagon**
tram

20 **pedikab**
pedicab; trishaw

21 **pasahero**
passenger

22 **sumakay ng bus**
take a bus; by bus

23 **habulin ang biyahe ng bus**
catch a bus

24 **habulin ang biyahe ng tren**
catch a train

25 **sumakay ng tren**
ride a train

26 **magmaneho ng kotse**
drive a car

27 **sumakay ng bisikleta**
ride a bike

28 **bagalan**
slow down

29 **bilisan**
go faster

30 **kumaliwa/ kumanan**
turn left/ turn right

31 **dumiretso**
go straight

32 **iskedyul ng tren**
train schedule

33 **bilihan ng tiket**
ticket counter

34 **ruta ng bus**
bus route

35 **kalesa**
horse carriage

36 **tumawag ng taksi**
to call a taxi

37 **Grab**
Grab

38 **Anong pinakamagandang paraan papunta sa bayan o sentro?**
What is the best way to get downtown?

39 **Sumakay ka ng bus, taksi, o tren**
By bus, by taxi or take the train.

40 **Paano ako pupunta sa estasyon ng tren?**
How do I get to the train station?

13 | Pagtatanong at Pagbibigay ng Direksyon
Asking and Giving Directions

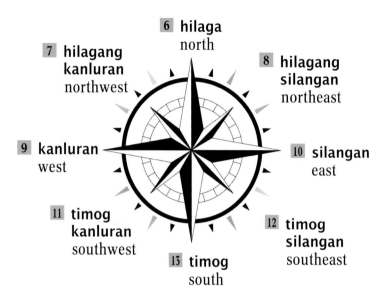

6 hilaga
north

7 hilagang kanluran
northwest

8 hilagang silangan
northeast

9 kanluran
west

10 silangan
east

11 timog kanluran
southwest

12 timog silangan
southeast

13 timog
south

14 sa harap
in front

15 sa likod
behind

1 saan?
where?

2 dito
here

3 doon
there

4 sa ibabaw
above

5 sa ilalim
below

Some common phrases for asking and giving directions:

16 pagtatanong ng direksyon
asking directions

21 pagbibigay ng direksyon
giving directions

17 Nawawala ako. Puwede mo ba akong tulungan?
I'm lost. Can you help me?

18 Ito ba ang daan papunta sa...?
Is this the way to … ?

19 Gaano kalayo ang...?
How far is it?

20 Puwede mo ba ipakita kung nasaan ako sa mapa?
Can you show me on the map?

22 Paumanhin, hindi ko alam.
I'm sorry, I don't know.

23 Dito ang daan.
It's this way.

24 Doon ang daan.
It's that way.

25 Nasa kaliwa/kanan ito.
It's on the left/right.

26 Katabi ito ng...
It's next to … .

28 sa gitna
middle; center

27 sa kanang bahagi
right side

29 sa kaliwang bahagi
left side

30 lumiko sa kaliwa
turn left

31 dumiretso
go straight

32 lumiko sa kanan
turn right

33 sa labas
outside

34 sa loob
inside

Additional Vocabulary

35 mawala
to be lost

36 direksyon
direction

37 layo
distance

38 kilometro
kilometer

39 milya
mile

40 metro
meter

41 talampakan
foot

42 malapit
near

43 malayo
far

44 kabaliktaran
opposite

45 sa Silangan
the East

46 sa Timog
the South

47 sa Kanluran
the West

48 sa Hilaga
the North

49 bahagi
side

50 malapit
nearby

51 lugar
place

52 sa isang bahagi
one side

53 sabihin
to tell

54 dumaan
to go through

55 umalis
to leave

56 gaano pa katagal?
how much longer?

57 kaagad
immediately

58 payagan
to allow

59 na
already

60 mag-isip
to think

61 isaalang-alang
to consider

62 tumulong
to help

63 mabalisa
to feel anxious

14 | Usapang Panahon
Talking About the Weather

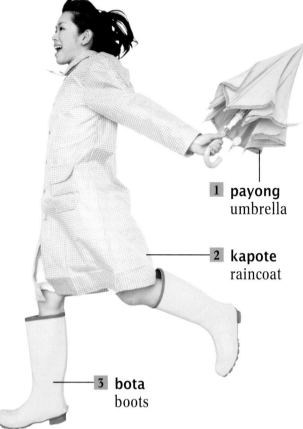

1 payong
umbrella

2 kapote
raincoat

3 bota
boots

4 maaliwalas
clear (sky)

5 maaliwalas na araw
clear day

6 maulap
overcast

7 makulimlim
cloudy day

8 hangin
wind

9 mahangin
windy

10 ulan
rain

11 umuulan
raining

12 kidlat
lightning

13 kulog
thunder

14 ulan at pag-kulog
thunderstorm

15 niyebe
snow

16 magniyebe
to snow

17 bagyo
typhoon

41 Maganda ang araw ngayon. Uulan bukas.
It's a beautiful day today. Tomorrow will be rainy.

42 Napakainit ngayon. Mas malamig bukas.
It is too hot today. Tomorrow will be cooler.

36

18 jaket
coat or jacket

19 sweter
sweater

Additional Vocabulary

32 panahon
weather

33 ulat ng panahon
weather forecast

34 mabuting panahon
good weather

35 masamang panahon
bad weather

36 maaraw
sunny weather

37 polusyon sa hangin
air pollution

38 ipo-ipo
hurricane

39 damit panlamig
cold weather clothes

40 damit pantag-araw
hot weather clothes

20 mainit
hot

21 mainit na panahon
hot weather

22 malamig
cold

23 malamig na panahon
cold weather

24 mga ulap
clouds

25 hamog
fog

26 araw
sun

27 buwan
moon

30 sombrero
hat

28 bagyong malakas ang pag-ulan
rainstorm

29 ulan-yelo
hail

31 guwantes
gloves

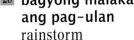

37

1 oras
hour

2 minuto
minute

3 segundo
second

6 orasan
clock

4 alas-sais
6 o'clock

5 singko minutos
pasado alas-sais
five minutes
past six

8 kinse minutos pasa-
do alas-sais
fifteen minutes past six

9 kalahating oras
pasado alas-sais
half past six

7 kinse
minutos
quarter
(hour)

10 kinse minutos
bago mag-
alas-siyete
fifteen minutes to
seven

11 singko minutos
bago mag-alas-
siyete
five minutes to
seven

37 Anong oras na?
What's the time?

38 Kalahating oras
pasado alas-otso
Half past eight.

39 Paumanhin, nahuli ako.
Sorry, I'm late.

40 Okey lang.
It's OK.

12 orasang may alarm
alarm clock

13 segundo-metro
stopwatch

14 smartwatch
smartwatch

15 relo
wrist watch

17 oras
time

18 madaling araw
early morning

19 ng umaga
in the morning; a.m.

20 tanghali
noon

21 ng hapon
in the afternoon; p.m.

22 hatinggabi
midnight

23 laging nasa oras
punctual

24 maaga
early

25 huli
late

26 alas-
o'clock

27 mamaya
later

28 bago
before

29 pagitan
between; among

30 sandaling panahon
a brief moment

31 kanina lang
a moment ago

32 noong nakaraan
(in the) past

33 madalas
frequently

34 sa madaling panahon
in a moment

35 bigla
sudden

36 sa wakas
finally

41 Magkita tayo ng alas-tres ng hapon.
See you at 3 p.m.!

16 gabi
night

16 Mga Taon at Petsa
Years and Dates

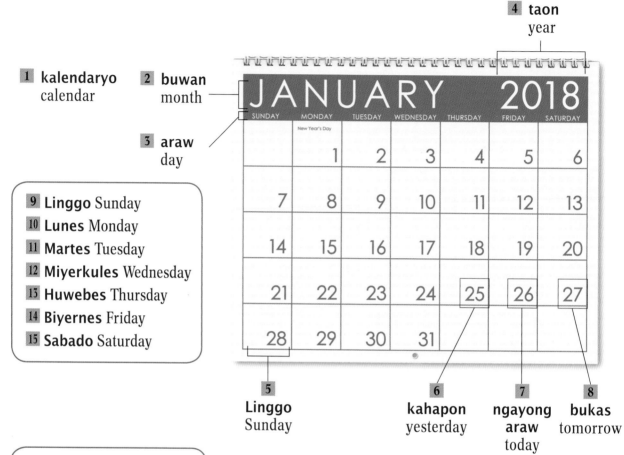

4 taon
year

1 kalendaryo
calendar

2 buwan
month

3 araw
day

JANUARY 2018

SUNDAY MONDAY TUESDAY WEDNESDAY THURSDAY FRIDAY SATURDAY

New Year's Day

9 **Linggo** Sunday
10 **Lunes** Monday
11 **Martes** Tuesday
12 **Miyerkules** Wednesday
13 **Huwebes** Thursday
14 **Biyernes** Friday
15 **Sabado** Saturday

5
Linggo
Sunday

6
kahapon
yesterday

7
ngayong
araw
today

8
bukas
tomorrow

45 **Gusto kong gumamit ng talaarawan.**
I like to keep a diary.

46 **Biyernes ngayon, ikadalawampu't anim ng Enero.**
Today is Friday, January 26.

47 **Huwebes kahapon, ikadalawampu't lima ng Enero.**
Yesterday was Thursday, January 25.

48 **Sabado bukas, ikadalawampu't pito ng Enero.**
Tomorrow will be Saturday, January 27.

How to express years, months and dates in Tagalog:

2017 is **Taong dawalang libo at labimpito**

2000 is **Taong dalawang libo**

1994 is **Taong isang libo siyam na raan at siyamnapu't apat**

2013 is **Taong dalawang libo at labintatlo**

The 12 months of the year in Tagalog are:

16 January **Enero**

17 February **Pebrero**

18 March **Marso**

19 April **Abril**

20 May **Mayo**

21 June **Hunyo**

22 July **Hulyo**

23 August **Agosto**

24 September **Setyembre**

25 October **Oktubre**

26 November **Nobyembre**

27 December **Disyembre**

Examples:

February 5	ikalima ng Pebrero
March 31	ikatatlumpu't isa ng Marso
April 1	ika-isa ng Abril
July 4	ika-apat ng Hulyo
December 25	ikadalawampu't lima ng Disyembre

49 **Kailan ang kaarawan mo?**
When is your birthday?

50 **Sa ikatatlumpu't isa ng Enero ang kaarawan ko.**
My birthday is on January 31.

Additional Vocabulary

28 **noong nakaraang taon**
last year

29 **noong isang taon**
the year before

30 **ngayong taon**
this year

31 **sa susunod na taon**
next year

32 **taon matapos ang susunod na taon**
the year after next

33 **linggo**
week

34 **taong gulang**
years (of age)

35 **taong bisyesto**
leap year

36 **araw sa isang buwan**
day of a month

37 **dekada**
decade (10 years)

38 **siglo**
century (100 years)

39 **milenyo**
millennium (1000 years)

40 **noong nakaraang linggo**
last week

41 **noong nakaraang buwan**
last month

42 **sa susunod na linggo**
next week

43 **sa susunod na buwan**
next month

44 **talaarawan**
diary

17 Mga Panahon ng Taon
The Seasons of the Year

1 tagsibol
spring

2 tag-araw
summer

3 taglagas
autumn; fall

4 taglamig
winter

5 mainit-init
warm

6 banayad na hangin
a gentle breeze

7 bulaklak
flower

8 mamulaklak
to flower

9 umambon
to drizzle

10 lilim
sun shade

11 basaan
water play

12 gumawa ng taong-niyebe
to make a snowman

Ang pagbabago ng mga kulay ng panahon.
The changing colors of the seasons.

| pamumulaklak | halaman sa tag-araw | paglalagas ng mga dahon | pagniniyebe |
| spring blossoms | summer greenery | autumn foliage | winter snow |

13 mag-ani
to harvest

14 pamaypay
fan

15 batuhan ng bola ng niyebe
snowball fights

16 pamahid na panlaban sa araw
sunblock lotion

17 pananim
crops

21 Gusto kong pumunta sa tabing-dagat at maglaro sa labas.
I like to go to the beach and play outdoors.

Additional Vocabulary

18 apat na panahon
four seasons

19 dati
before

20 sa totoo lang
actually

22 Ilang panahon mayroon sa isang taon?
How many seasons are there in a year?

23 May apat na panahon sa isang taon.
There are four seasons in a year.

24 Ano ang pinakagusto mong panahon?
Which season do you like best?

25 Tag-araw ang paborito kong panahon.
My favorite season is summer.

18 | Pagdiriwang ng mga Espesyal na Araw
Celebrating the Holidays

 **1** pista; pagdiriwang
festival; holiday

 **2** Bagong Taon
New Year

 **3** paputok
fireworks

 **4** Unang Araw ng Bagong Taon
New Year's Day

 **5** Araw ng mga Santo
All Saints' Day

 **6** Araw ng mga Patay
All Souls' Day

 **7** Bagong Taon ng mga Tsino
Spring Festival (Chinese New Year)

 **8** Pista ng mga Parol
Lantern Festival

 **9** Semana Santa Mahal na Araw
Holy Week

 **10** Araw ng mga Bayani
National Heroes Day

 **11** tikoy
Chinese New Year's Cake

 **12** Araw ng mga Tatay
Father's Day

 **13** Araw ng mga Nanay
Mother's Day

 **14** Araw ni Rizal
Rizal Day

44

15 Araw ng mga Puso
Valentine's Day

16 mga tsokolate
chocolates

17 mga rosas
roses

18 Araw ng Pasasalamat
Thanksgiving

19 bisperas ng Todos los Santos
Halloween

20 Araw ng Pagkabuhay
Easter

21 Araw ng Kalayaan
Independence Day

22 Pista ng Panagbenga
Flower Festival

23 Pista ng Nazareno
Feast of the Nazarene

27 kaarawan
birthday

28 dumalo sa salo-salo para sa kaarawan
attend a birthday party

29 bakasyon para sa tag-araw
summer vacation

30 bakasyon para sa taglamig
winter vacation

31 mga araw na walang pasok sa eskuwela
school holidays

32 anibersaryo
anniversary

33 Araw para sa mga nag-iisa
Singles' Day

34 salusalo
banquet; reception

35 kakanin
rice dumplings

36 Maligayang Kaarawan
Happy birthday!

24 regalo
gift

37 Maligayang Pasko!
Merry Christmas!

25 Pasko
Christmas

26 Santa Klaws
Santa Claus

38 Saluhan niyo kami sa pagdiwang ng Pasko.
Please join us for the Christmas celebrations.

45

19 Gustong-gusto kong Matuto
I Love to Learn

1 **eksamen**
exams

2 **pagbabasa**
reading

3 **pag-aaral**
to learn; to study

4 **matematika**
mathematics

5 **edukasyong pangkalusugan**
physical education

6 **sumagot**
to answer

7 **libro**
book

8 **ang balita**
the news

9 **diyaryo**
newspaper

10 **magasin**
magazine

12 **sulat**
letter

11 **diksyunaryo**
dictionary

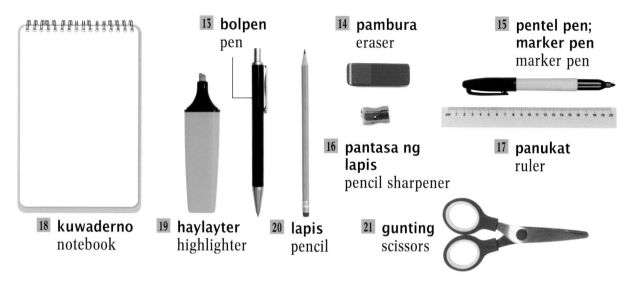

13 **bolpen**
pen

14 **pambura**
eraser

15 **pentel pen;**
marker pen
marker pen

16 **pantasa ng**
lapis
pencil sharpener

17 **panukat**
ruler

18 **kuwaderno**
notebook

19 **haylayter**
highlighter

20 **lapis**
pencil

21 **gunting**
scissors

Additional Vocabulary

22 **baitang;**
klase
grade; class

23 **maintindihan**
to understand

24 **mag-ensayo**
to practice

25 **magbalik-**
aral
to review

26 **tanong;**
problema
a question;
problem

27 **gawaing**
bahay
homework

28 **panitikan;**
literatura
literature

29 **kasaysayan**
history

30 **salita**
word

31 **kuwento**
story

32 **takdang**
aralin
assignment

33 **pag-ibig**
love

34 **heyometriya**
geometry

35 **agham**
science

36 **araling**
panlipunan
social studies

37 **ekonomika**
economics

38 **alhebra**
algebra

39 **pisika**
physics

40 **kemistri**
chemistry

41 **biyolohiya**
biology

42 **kalkulus**
calculus

43 **heyograpiya**
geography

44 **pagsusulit**
test

45 **talento;**
kakayahan
talent; ability

46 **masipag;**
seryoso
conscientious;
serious

47 **antas ng**
narating
level (of
achievement)

48 **gumaling**
to improve

49 **pinakama-**
galing
top; extreme

50 **maintindihan**
to understand

51 **pakay**
purpose

52 **Gustong-gusto ko ng mga libro!**
I love books!

53 **Ano ang paborito mong asignatura?**
What is your favorite subject?

54 **Gusto ko ang panitikan at kasaysayan.**
I like literature and history.

1 **puting pisara**
whiteboard

2 **blakbord; itim na pisara**
blackboard

3 **aklatan**
library

4 **silid-aralan;**
klasrum
classroom

5 **magturo**
to teach

6 **guro; titser**
teacher

7 **seroksan**
photocopier

8 **ipa-seroks**
to photocopy

9 **itaas ang kamay**
raise your hand

12 **agham**
science

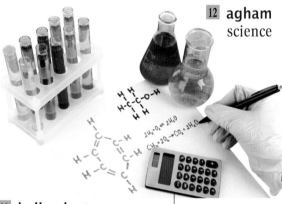

10 **propesor**
professor

11 **kalkyuleytor**
calculator

51 **Kailangan mo ba ng tulong sa iyong**
takdang aralin?
Do you need help with your homework?

13 **kaklase**
classmates

14 **silid-**
panayam
lecture hall

15 **estudyante**
student

16 paaralan; eskwelahan
school

17 punong guro
principal

18 awditoryum
auditorium

19 kompyuter lab
computer lab

20 laboratoryo
laboratory

21 alpabeto
alphabet

22 mga grado
grades

23 matalino
intelligent; clever

24 pribadong paaralan
private school

25 pampublikong paaralan
public school

26 teksbuk
textbook

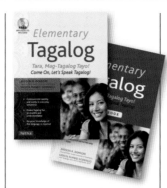

27 librong pansanay
workbook

28 paaralan para sa paunang elementarya
nursery school

29 pumasok sa elementarya
to attend elementary school

30 eskuwelahang pang–elementarya
elementary school

31 junior hayskul
middle school

32 senior hayskul
senior high school

33 unibersidad
university

34 kolehiyo
college

35 unang taon sa kolehiyo
freshman year in college

36 pangalawang taon sa kolehiyo
sophomore year in college

37 pangatlong taon sa kolehiyo
junior year in college

38 huling taon sa kolehiyo
senior year in college

39 klase sa gabi
night class

40 magpakadalub-hasa
to major

41 paksa
topic

42 dapat
must

43 rin; din
also

44 lumampas
to exceed

45 magtapos
to graduate

46 Nasa anong taon ka na?
What year are you?

47 Nasa ikalawang taon na ako sa kolehiyo
I'm a sophomore in college.

48 Nagpapakadalubhasa ako sa matematika.
I'm majoring in math.

49 Anong kurso mo?
What is your major?

50 Napakatalino mo siguro!
You must be very smart!

21 Pag-aaral ng Tagalog
Learning Tagalog

1 **Hindi mahirap matutunan ang wikang Filipino.**
Tagalog is not a difficult language to learn.

2 **isulat**
to write

3 **aklat sa pag sasanay**
exercise book

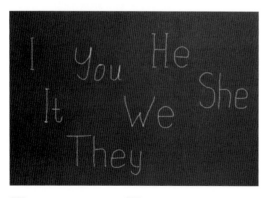

4 **panghalip**
pronoun

5 **ako**
I

6 **ikaw**
you

7 **siya**
he; she

8 **kami (exclusive); tayo (inclusive)**
we

9 **kayo**
you all

10 **sila**
they

11 **Madali!**
Easy!

12 **Mahirap!**
Difficult!

17 wikang Filipino
Filipino language

18 Taglish
Tagalog-English mix

19 talasalitaan
vocabulary

20 mag-aral
to study

21 matuto
to learn

22 bigkasin
to pronounce

23 basahin
to read

24 baybayin
to spell

25 magsanay
to practice

26 ulitin
to repeat

27 magsanay
to drill

28 magpursigi
to strive

29 maghanda
to prepare

30 maintindihan
to understand

31 pangungusap
sentence

32 parirala
phrase

33 sanaysay
essay

34 tula
poem

35 kultura
culture

36 gramatika
grammar

37 pagsasalin
translation

38 lingguwistika
linguistics

39 aralin
lesson

40 kurso; programang pang-akademiko
course; academic program

41 takdang aralin
assignment

42 tama
correct

43 mali
wrong

44 kahulugan
meaning

45 mga salita
words

46 pakiulit
please repeat

47 pakibilisan
please go fast

48 pakibagalan
please go slow

49 paki-sulat
please write it

50 paki-salin
please translate

51 magsalita
speak

52 sauluhin
memorize

53 kanta
song

54 maikling kuwento
short story

55 nobela
novel

56 aralin
lesson

57 pag-unawa
comprehension

58 pagbigkas
pronunciation

13 tandang padamdam
exclamation mark

14 tandang pananong
question mark

15 tuldok
period

16 kuwit
comma

Pareho ang Baybay, Magkaibang Tuldik, Magkaibang Kahulugan

22 | Filipino Accents—Same Spelling, Different Accents, Different Meanings

Ang isang salita ay puwedeng magkaroon ng dalawang kahulugan depende sa tuldik.
One word can have two meanings depending on the accent.

1 bába/babâ

chin

downstairs

2 upô/ùpo

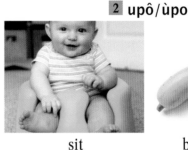

sit

bottle gourd

3 basâ/bása

wet

read

4 punô/pùno

full

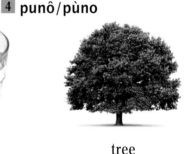

tree

5 kíta/kitá

profit

you (by me)

6 tíra/tirá

shoot!

leftover

7 píto/pitó

whistle

seven

8 páso/pasò

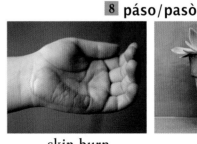

skin burn

pot

9 kápa/kapâ

cape

physically inspect

10 kaibígan/káibigan

friend

lover

11 táyo/tayò

us

stand up

12 bánda/bandá

band

area; side

Additional Vocabulary

13 pála/palá
shovel/(surprise marker)

14 sayá/sáya
fun/Filipino dress made in Pina

15 píli/pilî
choice/chosen

16 pása/pasá
pass/bruise

17 datìng/dáting
demeanor/former

18 sikát/síkat
famous/shine

19 tubò/tùbo
sugar cane/profit

20 báka/baká
cow/might

21 Mag-ensayo táyo.
Let us practice.

22 May pitòng pìto si Pedro.
Pedro has seven whistles.

23 Bakà mahal ang bàka sa palengke.
The cow might be expensive at the market.

24 Malaki ang tùbo sa pagbebenta ng tubò.
Selling sugarcane is profitable.

25 Malakas pa rin ang datìng ng dàting sikat na artista na si Pepe.
Former actor Pepe still has a strong presence.

26 Ang sayà magsuot ng sàya tuwing piyesta.
It is fun to wear the *saya* during feast.

27 Ikaw palà ang nagnakaw ng pàla!
So you are the one who stole the shovel!

23 Mga Kompyuter at ang Internet
Computers and the Internet

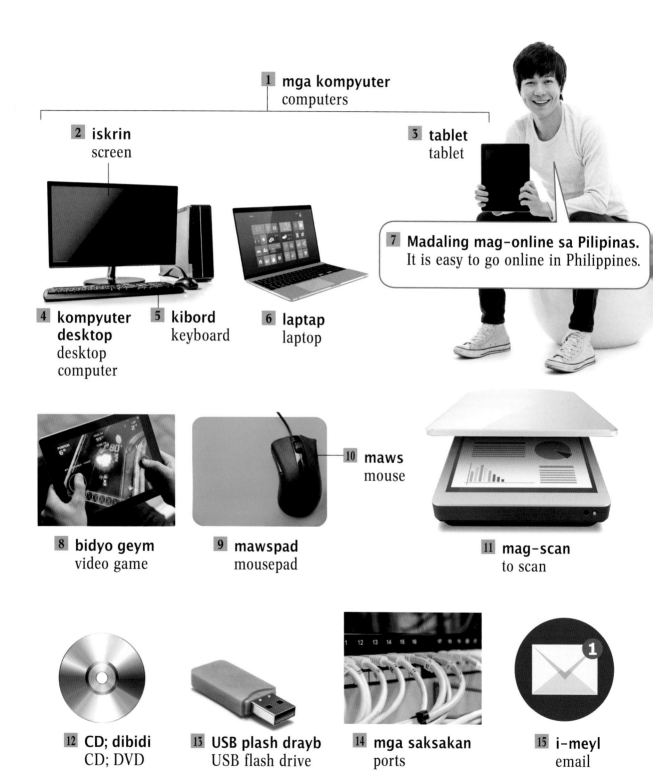

1 mga kompyuter
computers

2 iskrin
screen

3 tablet
tablet

7 Madaling mag-online sa Pilipinas.
It is easy to go online in Philippines.

4 kompyuter desktop
desktop computer

5 kibord
keyboard

6 laptap
laptop

8 bidyo geym
video game

9 mawspad
mousepad

10 maws
mouse

11 mag-scan
to scan

12 CD; dibidi
CD; DVD

13 USB plash drayb
USB flash drive

14 mga saksakan
ports

15 i-meyl
email

16 internetan
internet shop

17 bayad kada oras
hourly rate

18 magsurf
to surf

19 maglaro
to play

20 magpaprint
to print

21 magpakopya
to photocopy

22 i-click
to click

23 i-download
to download

24 i-upload
to upload

25 i-update
to update

26 mag-onlayn
to go online

27 magchat
to chat

28 magpost
to post

29 magsayn-in
to sign in

30 magpalit; magbago
to change

31 pasword
password

32 mga larawan
pictures

33 websayt
website

34 Mag-online ka
Go online

35 mabagal ang koneksyon ng internet
slow internet connection

36 mabilis mag-upload
fast to upload

37 madaling gamitin
easy to use

38 mahirap maintindihan
hard to understand

39 maghanap online
online search

40 magpakabit ng internet sa bahay
get internet service at home

41 maghanap ng internetan
look for an internet cafe

42 bayrus
virus

43 payl
file

44 networking
networking

45 web adres
web address; URL

46 aplikeysyon
application (computer program)

47 pahina ng web
web page

48 disenyo ng websayt
web design

49 akses sa internet
internet access

50 ayon sa; ayon kay
according to

51 pagkatapos noon
after that

52 dahil
because

53 dagdag doon
in addition

54 Hilig ko ang *online gaming*.
My hobby is online gaming.

55 Magchat tayo onlayn.
Let's chat online.

56 Anong app ang ginagamit mo? WeChat ang gamit ko.
What app do you use? I use WeChat.

57 Sige, ipinapadala ko na ang mga dokumento sa kompyuter.
Okay, I'm now sending you the documents via computer.

24 Gustong-gusto ko ang Smartphone ko!
I Love My Smartphone!

1 smartphone
smartphone

2 mga kaibigan sa internet
online friends

3 mamili sa internet
online shopping

4 internetan
internet cafes

5 Twitter
Twitter

6 WeChat
WeChat

7 teleponong Android
Android phones

8 teleponong Apple
Apple phones (iPhones)

9 selfon
mobile phone

10 tawagan sa telepono
to make a phone call

11 makatang-gap ng tawag sa telepono
to receive a phone call

Additional Vocabulary

24 pagteteks
texting

25 wikang gamit sa internet
internet slang

26 pang-charge ng telepono
phone charger

27 kard para sa telepono
phone cards

28 long distance na tawag
long distance call

29 bidyo
video

30 SIM kard
SIM card

31 saksakan
outlet

32 lagayan ng selfon
phone case

33 aksesorya ng selfon
phone accessory

34 kable
cable

35 charger
charger

36 tindahan ng aksesorya ng selfon
mobile accessory shop

37 lobat; paubos na ang karga ng baterya
low battery

12 malakas ang signal
strong signal

13 mahina ang signal
weak signal

14 selfie; kunan ang sarili
selfie

15 wefie; kunan ang grupo
wefie

Some common telephone phrases:

38 Hello?/Ako si (pangalan).
Hello?/This is (name).

39 Maaari bang makausap si (pangalan)?
May I speak to (name)?

40 Pakisabi tawagan ako.
Please ask him/her to return my call.

41 Puwede ka bang makipag-usap ngayon?
Is it convenient to talk now?

42 Maaari mo bang lakasan ang boses mo?
Could you speak up?

43 Paumanhin, mali ang dinayal mong numero.
Sorry, you dialed the wrong number.

44 Sandali lang.
Please wait a moment.

45 Mag-iwan ka ng mensahe.
Please leave a message.

46 Sino ang tumatawag?
Who's calling, please?

47 Maaari mo bang bagalan ang pagsasalita?
Could you speak a little slower?

48 Puwede bang makuha ang numero mo sa selfon?
Can I get your mobile number?

49 Nakapatay ang selfon ko.
My mobile phone is off.

50 Saan ako puwedeng mag-charge ng selfon?
Where can I charge my mobile phone?

16 Olx
Olx

17 Lazada
Lazada

18 Facebook
Facebook

19 Google
Google

20 Shopee
Shopee

21 Viber
Viber

22 Apple
Apple

23 Microsoft
Microsoft

25 Sa Trabaho
At Work

9 **arkitekto**
architect

10 **opereytor ng telepono**
telephone operator

1 **abogado**
lawyer

2 **hukom; huwes**
judge

3 **tagapondo**
financier

4 **inhinyero**
engineer

15 **opisina**
office

5 **akawntant**
accountant

6 **parmasyutiko**
pharmacist

7 **alagad ng sining**
artist

8 **musikero**
musician

16 **manedyer; tagapamahala**
manager

17 **kalihim**
secretary

11 punong tagapagluto
chef

12 potograpo
photographer

13 piloto
pilot

14 dentista
dentist

18 bumbero
firefighter

19 magsasaka
farmer

Additional Vocabulary

20 kumpanya
company

21 negosyante
entrepreneur

22 inspeksyunin
to inspect

23 pumasok sa trabaho
going to work

24 kasama sa trabaho; katrabaho
colleague

25 trabaho
work

26 empleyado
employee

27 baguhan
apprentice

28 mag-intern
to intern

29 oras ng trabaho
shift work

30 panggabi
night shift

31 pang-umaga
morning shift

32 mag-obertaym
to work overtime

33 tagabigay ng serbisyo
service provider

34 paraan
method

35 oportunidad
opportunity

36 posisyon
position

37 palagi
always

38 Anong klase ang trabaho mo? Nagtatrabaho ako sa ospital.
What sort of work do you do? I work in a hospital.

39 Nagsasanay ako maging doktor.
I'm training to be a doctor.

40 Pumapasok ako sa trabaho ng 8:45 tuwing umaga.
I go to work at 8:45 a.m. every morning.

26 | Musika at Sayaw
Music and Dance

1 gitara
guitar

2 kulintang
small horizontally
laid gongs

3 pipa
pipa

4 biyolin
violin

5 sumayaw
to dance

6 tambol
drums

7 bandurya
bandurria

8 piyano
piano

9 trumpeta
trumpet

10 plauta
flute

11 karaoke; videoke
karaoke

12 kumanta
to sing

18 magustuhan
to appreciate;
to enjoy

19 musika at
sayaw
music and dance

20 sumayaw
dance
(performance art)

21 magtanghal
to perform

22 programa
program

23 musikang pop
pop music

24 tumugtog
to play a (string)
musical instru-
ment

25 earphones
earphones

26 musikang
klasikal
classical music

27 banda; orkestra
band; orchestra

28 mang–aawit
singer

29 hilig
hobby

30 sikat
famous

31 ipahayag
to express

32 artista;
aktor; aktres
artist; actor;
actress

13 konsiyerto
concert

14 manonood
audience

15 harana
serenade

16 tselo
cello

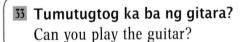

33 Tumutugtog ka ba ng gitara?
Can you play the guitar?

17 grupong pop
pop group

34 Anong klase ng musika ang
gusto mo?
What kind of music do you like?

27 | **Pagpunta sa Doktor**
Seeing a Doctor

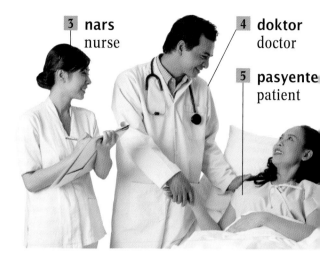

3 **nars**
nurse

4 **doktor**
doctor

5 **pasyente**
patient

1 **ospital**
hospital

2 **kuwartong pang-emerdyensi**
emergency room

6 **kumuha ng dugo**
to draw blood

7 **suriin ang dugo**
blood test

8 **pagsusuring laboratoryo**
laboratory test

9 **presyon sa dugo**
blood pressure

10 **magkasipon**
to catch a cold

11 **umubo**
to cough

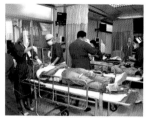

12 **lagnat**
fever

13 **magka-sakit**
to fall sick

14 **uminom ng gamot**
to take medicine

15 **gamot**
medicine

16 **pils**
pills

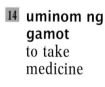

17 **iniksiyon**
injection

18 **silid-konsultas-yon ng doktor**
doctor's consulta-tion room

Additional Vocabulary

19 hintayan
waiting room

20 iskedyul
appointment

21 ambulansya
ambulance

22 pagdedentista
dentistry

23 pangkalahatang medisina
general medicine

24 pangkalahatang operasyon
general surgery

25 tenga, ilong at lalamunan
ear, nose, and throat

26 pedyatriya
pediatrics

27 ginekolohiya
gynecology

28 optalmolohiya
ophthalmology

29 dermatolohiya
dermatology

30 onkolohiya
oncology

31 terapyutikang pisikal
physiotherapy

32 nurolohiya
neurology

33 reydiyolohiya
radiology

34 aksidente
accident

35 preskripsyon
prescription

36 antiseptiko
antiseptic

37 pampahid
ointment

38 sugat
wound; cut

39 emerhensya
emergency

40 masakit
hurts

41 pagod
tired; worn out

42 maramdaman
to feel

43 mula
from

44 makailang beses
several times

45 nag-aalala
anxious; worried

46 malaman
to discover

47 manigurado
to feel reassured

48 mag-alala tungkol sa; kay
to be concerned about

49 tungkol sa; kay
pertaining to

50 sana; pag-asa
hope

51 importante; mahalaga
important

52 pangunahin
main

53 kit para sa pangunang lunas
first aid kit

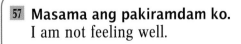

54 bendahe
bandage

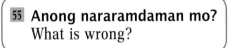

55 Anong nararamdaman mo?
What is wrong?

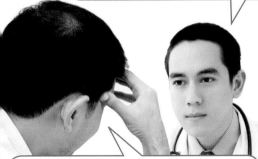

56 May lagnat ako at masakit ang lalamunan.
I have a fever and a sore throat.

57 Masama ang pakiramdam ko.
I am not feeling well.

58 Gusto kong kumunsulta sa doktor.
I would like to see a doctor.

59 Naka-iskedyul ka ba?
Do you have an appointment?

28 | **Pangangalaga sa Kalikasan**
Protecting Our Environment

1 hardin
garden

2 bulaklak
flower

3 parke
park

4 polusyon
pollution

5 damo
grass

6 kotseng de-kuryente
electric car

7 karagatan
ocean

8 ilog
river

9 enerhiyang mula sa araw
solar energy

10 tahimik
quiet

12 kuryenteng mula sa hangin
wind power

41 Napakasariwa ng hangin dito!
The air here is really fresh!

11 hangin
air

13 gubat
forest

15 natural na gas
natural gas

16 nukleyar na enerhiya
nuclear energy

14 puno
tree

42 Nag-recycle ka ba?
Do you recycle?

43 Inuulit ko ang paggamit ng baso, papel, at plastik.
I recycle glass, paper and plastic.

65

29 Kaharian ng mga Hayop
The Animal Kingdom

3 dyirap
giraffe

1 su
zoo

2 sibra
zebra

4 tigre
tiger

5 liyon
lion

39 Mas maliit ang hayop na ito kaysa doon sa isa.
This animal is smaller than that one.

40 Mahilig ka bang pumunta sa su?
Do you like going to the zoo?

41 Maraming mga hayop sa su.
There are many animals in the zoo.

10 dinosawro
dinosaur

6 oso
bear

7 unggoy
monkey

8 gorilya
gorilla

9 panda
panda

11 **kambing**
goat

12 **tupa**
sheep

13 **baka**
cow

Additional Vocabulary

29 **Napaka-**
How (wonderful; etc.)

30 **matakot**
to be afraid

31 **kyut; kahanga-hanga**
cute; adorable

32 **ito**
it

33 **sobrang; masyadong**
very; extremely

34 **pareho; magkatulad**
same; identical

35 **magkamukha**
to resemble

36 **magpakita**
to appear

37 **maglakas-loob**
to dare

38 **hindi karani-wan**
strange

14 **elepante**
elephant

15 **kabayo**
horse

16 **lobo**
wolf

17 **ahas**
snake

18 **pabo**
peacock

19 **manok**
chicken

20 **ibon**
bird

21 **aso**
dog

22 **pusa**
cat

23 **malmag**
Philippine tarsier

24 **lamok**
mosquito

25 **langaw**
housefly

26 **bubuyog**
bee

27 **paruparo**
butterfly

28 **isda**
fish

30 Maging Malusog tayo!
Let's Keep Fit!

1 pingpong
table tennis

2 mag-futbol
to play soccer

3 ragbi
rugby

**4 pag-akyat
sa bundok**
mountain
climbing

5 badminton
badminton

**6 mag-ehersisyo;
pampalakasan**
to exercise; sports

7 beysbol
baseball

9 pagtakbo
running

**10 malayuang
pagtakbo**
long-distance
running

11 bisikleta
bicycle

**8 mabilisang
takbuhan**
sprint

12 magbisikleta
to cycle

15 golp
golf

16 pag-iskeyt sa yelo
ice-skating

17 pag-iski
skiing

13 paligsahan
competition

14 katapusan ng linya
finish line

18 pagsasagwan
rowing

19 paglangoy
swimming

20 bolibol
volleyball

21 paglakad
walking

Additional Vocabulary

25 polong pang-isports
sports shirt;
sweatshirt

26 sapatos na pang-isports
sports shoes;
sneakers

27 bola
ball

28 malusog
healthy

22 tenis
tennis

23 raketa
racket

29 Gusto mo ba ang pag-eehersisyo?
Do you like to exercise?

30 Anong isports ang nilalaro mo?
What sports do you play?

31 Gusto ko ang pagtakbo at paglalaro ng basketbol.
I like to jog and play basketball.

24 maglaro ng basketbol
play basketball

31 Gusto mo bang Maglakbay?
Do You Like to Travel?

3 biyahero (male); biyahera (female)
traveler

4 bagahe
luggage

5 maleta
suitcase

1 otel
hotel

2 mapa
map

6 gabay sa paglilibot
tour guide

7 atraksyon para sa mga turista
tourist attraction

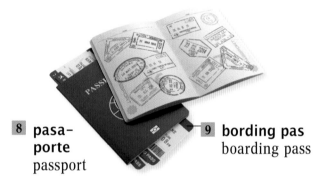

8 pasa-porte
passport

9 bording pas
boarding pass

10 magbiyahe sa-kay ng eroplano
travel by airplane

11 magbiyahe sakay ng tren
travel by rail

12 lakbay–dagat
on a cruise

13 nakabus
on a coach

14 bilihan ng pasalubong
souvenir shop

15 kamera
camera

16 larawan
photograph

70

Additional Vocabulary

17 biyahe; maglakbay
a trip; to travel

18 bakasyon
vacation

19 tiket sa eroplano
plane ticket

20 reserbasyon sa otel
hotel reservation

21 pera
currency

22 bisa
visa

23 librong gabay sa pagbibiyahe
travel guidebook

24 ahensya sa paglalakbay
travel agency

25 bakuna
vaccination

26 murang tuluyan
budget inn

27 kostoms
customs

28 pagliliwaliw
sightseeing

29 sentro ng impormasyon para sa turista
tourist information center

30 poskard
postcard

31 libreng *wifi*
free wifi

32 museo
museum

33 tabing-dagat; dalampasigan
beach

34 monumento
monument

35 istasyon ng tren
train station

36 paliparan
airport

37 sentro ng paglalayag
cruise center

38 tuluyan ng mga bisita
guesthouse; lodge

39 restawran; kainan
restaurant

40 maghanap
to find

41 magdala
to take

42 madaanan (thing; place); magkita (person)
to come across

43 ibalin ang atensyon
to pay attention to

44 maging mapag-matiyag; maging malay sa
to become aware of

45 sa iba
another

46 iba
others

47 baka
maybe

48 Saan mo gustong magbakasyon?
Where do you like to go on vacation?

49 Gusto kong pumunta sa Pampanga.
I like to go to Pampanga.

50 Gusto ko ng pabalik na tiket papuntang Taft.
I'd like a return train ticket to Taft.

51 Nilibot niya ang buong mundo.
He made a round-the-world trip.

52 Gusto kong lumipad sa parehong airline para makakuha ng puntos sa milya.
I like to fly on the same airline to get mileage points.

32 Mga Bansa sa Mundo at ang Gobyerno
Countries of the World and the Government

1 Mga bansa sa Timog-Siliangan Asya
Countries in Southeast Asia

2 Pilipinas
Philippines

3 Tsina
China

4 Koreya
Korea

5 Amerika
America

6 Alemanya
Germany

7 Britanya
Great Britain

8 Bansang Hapon
Japan

9 Rusiya
Russia

11 Pitong kontinente ng mundo
Seven continents of the world

10 Italya
Italy

16 Asya
Asia

12 Hilagang Amerika
North America

13 Timog Amerika
South America

14 Aprika
Africa

15 Europa
Europe

17 Australya
Australia

18 Antartika
Antartica

19 Gusto naming idaos ang seremonya ng aming kasal sa Pilipinas.
We intend to hold our wedding ceremony in the Philippines.

20 Sa anong bansa ka galing? Amerikano ako.
What country are you from? I am American.

Additional Vocabulary

21 daigdig
globe

22 mundo
world

23 **Kagawaran ng Edukasyon** Department of Education
24 **Kagawaran ng Kalusugan** Department of Health
25 **Kagawaran ng Repormang Pansakahan** Deparment of Agrarian Reform
26 **Kagawaran ng Pagsasaka** Department of Agriculture
27 **Kagawaran ng Pagbabadyet at Pamamahala** Department of Budget and Management
28 **Kagawaran ng Enerhiya** Department of Energy
29 **Kagawaran ng Kapaligiran at Likas na Yaman** Department of Environment and Natural Resources
30 **Kagawaran ng Pananalapi** Department of Finance
31 **Kagawaran ng Ugnayang Panlabas** Department of Foreign Affairs
32 **Kagawaran ng Interyor at Pamahalaang Lokal** Department of the Interior and Local Government
33 **Kagawaran ng Katarungan** Department of Justice
34 **Kagawaran ng Paggawa at Empleyo** Department of Labor and Employment
35 **Kagawaran ng Tanggulang Pambansa** Department of National Defense
36 **Kagawaran ng Pagawaing Bayan at Lansangan** Department of Public Works and Highways
37 **Kagawaran ng Agham at Teknolohiya** Department of Science Technology
38 **Kagawaran ng Kalingang Panlipunan at Pagpapaunlad** Department of Social Welfare and Development
39 **Kagawaran ng Turismo** Department of Tourism
40 **Kagawaran ng Kalakalan at Industriya** Department of Trade and Industry
41 **Kagawaran ng Transportasyon** Department of Transportation
42 **Lehislatibong Sangay** Legislative Branch
43 **Kongreso/Mababang Kapulungan** Congress/Lower Chamber
44 **Senado/Mataas na Kapulungan** Senate/Higher Chamber
45 **Kapulungan ng mga Kinatawan** House of Representatives
46 **Korte Suprema/Kataas-taasang Hukuman** Supreme Court
47 **Gobyerno** Government
48 **konstitusyon** Constitution
49 **pulitika** politics
50 **Ehekutibong Sangay** Executive Branch
51 **presidente** President
52 **bise presidente** Vice President
53 **gabinete** cabinet
54 **kagawaran** department
55 **kalihim** Department Secretary
56 **Senador** Senator
57 **kongresista** Congressman/woman
58 **batas** law
59 **Hudisyal na Sangay** Judicial Branch
60 **Punong Hukom** Chief Justice
61 **Mahistrado** Magistrate
62 **Pamahalaang Lokal** Local Government
63 **Gobernador** Governor
64 **Bise-Gobernador** Vice Governor
65 **Alkalde** Mayor
66 **Bise-Alkalde** Vice Mayor
67 **Konsehal** Councilor
68 **bansa** country
69 **rehiyon** region
70 **probinsya** province
71 **siyudad** city
72 **patakaran** rules
73 **regulasyon** regulations
74 **publiko** public
75 **Karapatan** Right
76 **eleksyon** election
77 **boto** vote
78 **panunumpa** oath
79 **pagpapatalsik** impeachment
80 **buwis** tax
81 **taripa** tariff
82 **korupsyon** corruption
83 **demokrasya** democracy
84 **Komunismo** Communism
85 **pasismo** facism
86 **sosyalismo** socialism
87 **monarkiya** monarchy
88 **totalitaryanismo** totalitarianism
89 **republikanismo** republicanism
90 **diktadura** dictatorship
91 **oligarkiya** oligarchy
92 **anarkismo** anarchism
93 **absolutismo** absolutism
94 **liberalismo** liberalism
95 **konserbatismo** conservatism
96 **progresibo** progressive
97 **imigrasyon** immigration
98 **pasaporte** passport
99 **bisa** visa

33 Mga Banyagang Wika
Foreign Languages

Guten Tag!

4 Aleman
German

Hello!

Bonjour!

привет

1 Ingles
English

2 Pranses
French

3 Ruso
Russian

Ciao!

¡Hola!

5 Italyano
Italian

6 Espanyol
Spanish

Merhaba!

こんにちは

مرحبا

7 Turko
Turkish

8 Hapon
Japanese

9 Arabe
Arabic

10 **Griyego**
Greek

11 **Hebreo**
Hebrew

12 **Vietnamese**
Vietnamese

13 **Hindi**
Hindi

14 **Indones**
Indonesian

15 **Tay**
Thai

16 **Koreyano**
Korean

17 **Tagalog**
Tagalog

18 **Portuges**
Portuguese

19 **Mandarin**
Mandarin
Chinese

20 **Ano ang iyong unang wika?**
What is your mother tongue?

21 **Ilang wika ang nasasalita mo?**
How many languages do you speak?

34 Gusto mo ba ng Pagkaing Filipino?
Do You Like Filipino Food?

1 restawrang Filipino
Filipino restaurant

2 weyter; tagasilbi
waiter; waitress

3 tagaluto
cook; chef

4 menyu
menu

5 adobo
pork and chicken cooked in soy sauce, vinegar and garlic

6 siomai
dimsum

7 sinangag
fried rice

8 tinapay
bread

9 tinola
chicken ginger stew

10 lumpia
Filipino spring roll made with vegetables

11 lechon
roasted suckling pig

12 tsapstiks
chopsticks

17 tinidor
fork

18 kutsilyo
knife

13 mangkok
bowl

14 kanin
cooked rice

16 plato
plate

15 puting kanin
white rice

19 kutsara
spoon

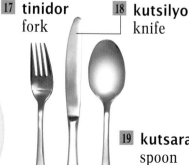

20 kare–kare
simmered oxtail and vegetables in peanut-based sauce

21 malamig na pampagana
cold dish (appetizer)

22 siopao
steamed bun

Additional Vocabulary

30 ulam
viand

31 agahan
breakfast

32 tanghalian
lunch

33 hapunan
dinner

34 sabaw
soup

35 walang karne
vegetarian

36 pili
choice

37 espesyal
special

38 rin; din
also; too

39 baka
perhaps

40 halos; muntik na
almost

41 tocino
sweet cured pork belly

42 longganisa
Filipino sausage

43 krispy pata
deep fried pork leg

44 bicol express
pork cubes in coconut milk and chili peppers

45 tapa
dried meat

23 sisig
Filipino dish made of chopped deep fried pork head skin and liver

24 pansit
noodles
25 kalamansi
native lime

26 pinasingawang isda
steamed fish

27 sinigang na baboy
sour soup made with pork ribs and vegetables

28 dinuguan
pork meat cooked in vinegar and pig's blood

29 champorado
sweet chocolate rice porridge

46 Mahilig ang lahat kumain ng pagkaing Filipino.
Everyone likes to eat Filipino food.

47 Iniimbita kita para sa hapunan mamayang gabi.
I'm inviting you for dinner tonight.

48 Maigi! Gusto kong kumain ng pagkaing Pilipino.
That's great! I want to eat Filipino food.

35 Mga Pagkaing Pangkalye at mga Panghimagas
Street Foods and Desserts

1 kwek kwek
orange-colored
batter deep-fried
quail eggs

2 balut
boiled duck-egg
embryo

3 bibingka
baked coconut
rice cake

4 helmet
grilled chicken
head

5 adidas
grilled chicken
feet

6 bananakyu
fried-sugared
banana

7 kikiyam
fish meat sausage

8 biko
sweet sticky rice

9 taho
fresh soft tofu
with sweetener,
and sago pearl

10 sago
tapioca pearl

11 puto bumbong
purple rice cake

12 halo-halo
shaved ice with
milk and mixed
fruits and beans

13 puto
steamed sweet rice
cake

14 butsi–butsi
deep fried sweet rice balls
covered in sesame seeds

15 suman
rice cooked in coco-
nut milk, wrapped
in coconut leaves

**16 ginataang halo–
halo**
glutinous rice balls
in coconut milk

17 keyk
cake

18 keso
cheese

19 halayang ube
purple yam

20 sorbetes
ice cream

**22 barbekyung
baboy**
pork barbecue

**23 barbekyung
manok**
chicken barbecue

24 isaw
grilled pig or
chicken intestine

25 penoy
duck egg

26 kamotekyu
sweet potato with
caramelized sugar
in sticks

27 turon
fried banana
rolls in caramel-
ized sugar

28 inihaw
grilled

29 pinirito
fried

30 nilaga
boiled

31 palitaw
sweet rice cake
covered in coco-
nut, sugar and
sesame

32 mais kon yelo
shaved ice with
corn kernel

33 gulaman
jelly

34 arnibal
caramelized
sugar

35 inihaw na mais
grilled corn

36 bayabas
guava

37 meryenda
snack

38 panghimagas
dessert

**39 mabigat sa
tiyan**
heavy meal

40 mabilis kainin
easy-to-eat

41 matagal maluto
slow-cook

42 tsitsaron
deep-fried pork
skin with salt

43 betamaks
grilled chicken
blood

21 letse flan
caramel
custard

Mga Inumin, Sariwang Prutas, Mani at katulad, at mga Butil
Drinks, Fresh Fruits, Nuts and Grains

1 mga inumin
beverage

2 tubig sa bote
mineral water

3 katas ng prutas
fruit juice

4 soya
soy milk

5 gatas
milk

6 kape
coffee

7 tsaa
tea

8 tsaang may yelo
iced tea

9 kok
cola

10 inuming pandiyeta
diet drinks

11 tubig mula sa gripo
tap water

12 tubig
water

13 uminom
to drink

14 uhaw
thirsty

15 inuming nagbibigay-enerhiya
energy drinks

16 inuming pang-isports
sports drinks

17 kakteyl
cocktails

19 puting bino
white wine

18 pulang bino
red wine

20 wiski
whiskey

21 syampeyn
Champagne

22 dilaw na bino
yellow wine

Additional Vocabulary

24 sopdringks
sodas

25 mainit na tubig
hot water

26 malamig na tubig
cold water

27 maliliit na yelo
ice cubes

28 tubig yelo
ice water

29 baso; tasa
glass; cup

30 bote
bottle

31 tapuy
rice wine

32 tuba
coconut flower wine

33 lambanog
coconut vodka

23 serbesa
beer

34 Ilang baso ng tubig ang dapat inumin ng tao araw-araw?
How many glasses of water should people drink every day?

35 Kung magmamaneho ka, huwag kang uminom. Kung iinom ka, huwag kang magmamaneho.
If you drive, don't drink. If you drink, don't drive.

36 Gusto kong uminom ng inuming mainit.
I want something hot to drink.

37 mansanas
apple

38 mangga
mango

39 kahel
orange

40 dalanghita
tangerine

41 peras
pear

42 niyog
coconut

43 saging
banana

44 pinya
pineapple

45 atis
custard apple

46 papaya
papaya

47 limon
lemon

48 kalamansi
lime

49 litsiyas
lychee

50 longgan
longan

51 presa
strawberry

52 ubas
grape

53 milong bilog
cantaloupe

54 persimon
persimmon

55 pakwan
watermelon

56 rambutan
rambutan

57 suha
grapefruit

58 kaymito
star apple

59 mangostin
mangosteen

60 manggang hilaw
raw mango

61 siniguwelas
Spanish plums

62 mani
peanuts

63 wolnat
walnuts

64 pekan
pecans

65 kastanyas
chestnuts

66 kasuy
cashew nuts

73 Puwedeng pahingi pa ng ensalada na walang mani?
Can I have one more salad without nuts?

67 butong pakwan
watermelon seeds

68 butong kalabasa
pumpkin seeds

69 obena
oats

Additional Vocabulary

78 siryal
grains; cereals

70 bigas
rice

71 trigo
wheat

72 linga
sesame seeds

79 mani
nuts

80 galyetas
crackers

81 nilugaw na obena
oatmeal

82 pinatuyong prutas
dried fruits

83 bins
beans

74 Anong klaseng mani ang gusto mo?
What nuts do you like?

75 Mahilig ako sa kasuy. Eh ikaw?
I like cashew nuts. What about you?

76 May alerji ako sa mani.
I am allergic to nuts.

84 mais
corn

85 arina
flour

86 may alerji sa
to be allergic; allergy

77 Gustong gusto kong kumain ng sariwang prutas.
I love to eat fresh fruits.

37 | Sa Palengke
At the Market

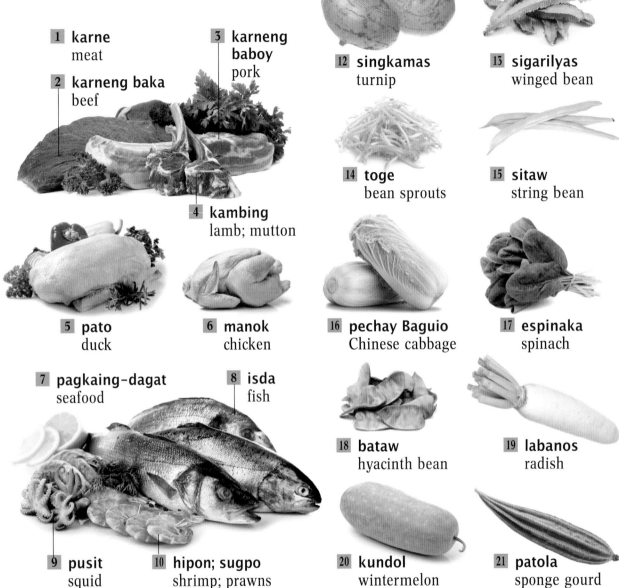

1 karne
meat

2 karneng baka
beef

3 karneng baboy
pork

4 kambing
lamb; mutton

5 pato
duck

6 manok
chicken

7 pagkaing-dagat
seafood

8 isda
fish

9 pusit
squid

10 hipon; sugpo
shrimp; prawns

11 mga gulay
vegetables

12 singkamas
turnip

13 sigarilyas
winged bean

14 toge
bean sprouts

15 sitaw
string bean

16 pechay Baguio
Chinese cabbage

17 espinaka
spinach

18 bataw
hyacinth bean

19 labanos
radish

20 kundol
wintermelon

21 patola
sponge gourd

---

64 Madaling lutuin ang pagkaing Filipino kapag mayroon ka lahat ng sangkap.
Filipino food is easy to cook once you have all the ingredients.

65 Sa Pilipinas, gusto naming bumili ng pagkain sa palengke.
In the Philippines, we like to buy our food at the local market.

66 Sariwang-sariwa ang karne at mga gulay doon. At medyo mas mura kaysa sa groseri.
The vegetables and meat are very fresh there. And it is slightly cheaper than the supermarket.

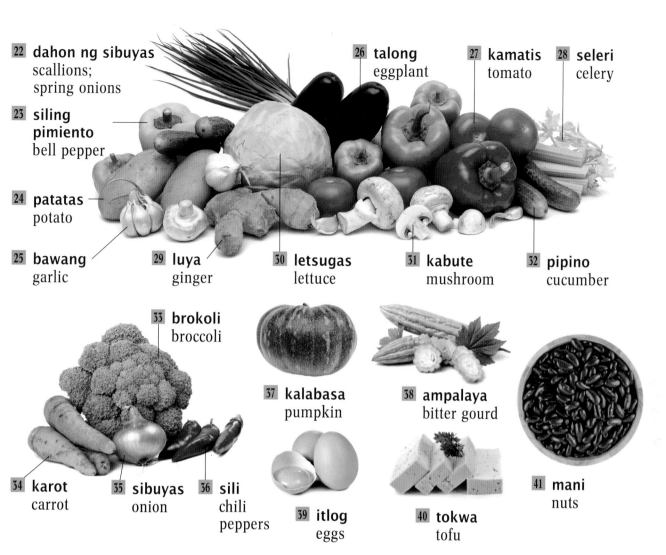

22 dahon ng sibuyas
scallions;
spring onions

23 siling pimiento
bell pepper

24 patatas
potato

25 bawang
garlic

26 talong
eggplant

27 kamatis
tomato

28 seleri
celery

29 luya
ginger

30 letsugas
lettuce

31 kabute
mushroom

32 pipino
cucumber

33 brokoli
broccoli

37 kalabasa
pumpkin

38 ampalaya
bitter gourd

34 karot
carrot

35 sibuyas
onion

36 sili
chili peppers

39 itlog
eggs

40 tokwa
tofu

41 mani
nuts

Additional Vocabulary

42 palengke
market

43 repolyo
cabbage

44 koliplor
cauliflower

45 patani
lima beans

46 upo
bottle gourd

47 giniling na baka
ground/minced
beef

48 giniling na baboy
ground/minced
pork

49 uri ng karne
types of meat

50 sariwa
fresh

51 pampalasa; rekado
seasonings

52 toyo
soy sauce

53 suka
vinegar

54 patis
fish sauce

55 bagoong
shrimp paste

56 asin
salt

57 betsin
monosodium
glutamate (MSG)

58 pulbos ng kari
curry powder

59 arina
starch

60 mantika
cooking oil

61 langis ng mani
peanut oil

62 langis ng niyog
coconut oil

63 pamintang durog
ground pepper

38 Mga Anyo ng Lupa at ang Gubat
Landforms and the Forest

1 bundok
mountain

2 bulkan
volcano

3 kapuluan
archipelago

4 gubat
forest

5 dahon
leaf

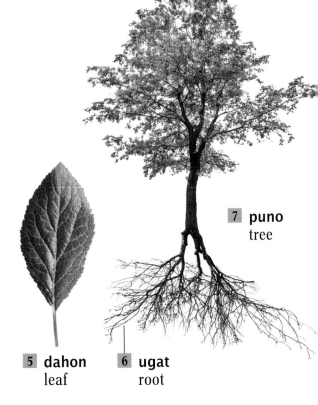

7 puno
tree

6 ugat
root

8 kuweba
cave

9 burol
hills

10 hagdan–hagdang palayan
rice terraces

11 baging
vine

12 kumukulong putik
lava

13 sunog sa gubat
forest fire

14 siga
bonfire

15 madamo
grassy

16 lawin
hawk

17 maputik
muddy

18 paniki
bat

22 uwak
raven

19 agila
eagle

20 kuwago
owl

21 kuneho
rabbit

Additional Vocabulary

23 lambak
valley

24 bulubundukin
mountain range

25 talampas
plateau

26 patag
plain

27 isla
island

28 tuktok
summit

29 mabato
rocky

30 madulas
slippery

31 kumunoy
quicksand

32 putik
mud

33 liblib (na lugar)
remote (place)

34 mapanganib
dangerous

35 makamandag
poisonous

36 Gusto kong maabot ang tuktok ng bundok.
I want to reach the mountain's summit.

37 Mag-ingat sa makamandag na mga halaman at mga hayop.
Be careful with poisonous plants and animals.

38 Tingnan ang nilalakaran ninyo. Madulas dito.
Watch your steps. It is slippery around here.

39 Mayroon pitong libo isang daan at pitong isla ang Pilipinas.
The Philippines has 7,107 islands.

1 **ilog**
river

2 **lawa**
lake

3 **balyena**
whale

6 **pating**
shark

4 **talon**
falls

5 **bukal**
spring

7 **buwaya**
crocodile

10 **pugita**
octopus

8 **dalampasigan**
beach

9 **masahe**
massage

11 **alimango**
crab

12 **hipon**
shrimp

13 **koral**
coral

14 **perlas**
pearl

15 **dikya**
jelly fish

16 **isda**
fish

17 **pusit**
squid

18 **tahong**
mussel

19 **kabibe**
clams

20 salbabida
life jacket

21 tsinelas
slippers

22 sarong
wrap around
cloth

23 duyan
hammock

Additional Vocabulary

24 karagatan
ocean

25 dagat
sea

26 tubig-dagat
seawater

27 sariwang tubig
freshwater

28 alon
beach wave

29 buhangin
sand

30 puting buhangin
white sand

31 kubo
hut

32 langis
oil

33 kulambo
mosquito net

34 May bakanteng kubo ba?
Is there a vacant hut?

35 Gusto kong gumawa ng kastilyong buhangin.
I want to make a sand castle.

36 Hindi ako marunong lumangoy.
I do not know how to swim.

37 Nalulunod ako! Saklolo! (alt. Tulong!)
I'm drowning! I need help!

38 Kailangan ko ng salbabida.
I need a lifevest.

39 Gusto kong makakita ng mga isda at mga balyena.
I want to see fishes and whales.

40 Gusto kong kumain ng alimango at hipon para sa hapunan.
I want to eat lobster and shrimp for dinner.

41 Ang linaw-linaw ng tubig.
The water is so clear.

42 Sobrang ganda. Gusto kong tumira sa Pilipinas.
It is so beautiful. I want to live in the Philippines.

English–Tagalog Index

1 cent **isang sentimo** [9–7] *26*
1 peso **isang piso; piso** [9–11] *26*
5 cents **limang sentimo** [9–6] *26*
5 pesos **limang piso** [9–12] *26*
6 o'clock **alas-sais** [15–4] *38*
10 cents **sampung sentimo** [9–5] *26*
10 pesos **sampung piso** [9–13] *26*
20 pesos **dalawampung piso** [9–14] *26*
25 cents **dalawampu't limang sentimo** [9–4] *26*
50 pesos **limampung piso** [9–15] *26*
100 pesos **isang daang piso** [9–16] *26*
500 pesos **limandaang piso** [9–17] *26*
1000 pesos **isanlibong piso** [9–18] *26*

A

a brief moment **sandaling panahon** [15–30] *39*
a circle **bilog** [7–19] *23*
a diamond **dyamante** [7–28] *23*
a gentle breeze **banayad na hangin** [17–6] *42*
a heart **puso** [7–23] *23*
a hexagon **heksagon; animang-sulok** [7–27] *23*
a moment ago **kanina lang** [15–31] *39*
a pentagon **pentagon; limahang-sulok** [7–21] *23*
a question; problem **tanong; problema** [19–26] *47*
a rainbow **bahaghari** [7–17] *22*
a rectangle **parihaba** [7–18] *23*
a square **parisukat** [7–22] *23*
a star **bituin** [7–25] *23*
a triangle **tatsulok** [7–26] *23*
a trip; to travel **biyahe; maglakbay** [31–17] *71*
abdomen **tiyan** [4–27] *17*
above **sa ibabaw** [13–4] *34*
accident **aksidente** [27–34] *63*
according to **ayon sa; ayon kay** [23–50] *55*
account number **numero ng akawnt** [9–34] *27*
accountant **akawntant** [25–5] *58*
actually **sa totoo lang** [17–20] *43*
after that **pagkatapos noon** [23–51] *55*
Africa **Aprika** [32–14] *72*
air **hangin** [28–11] *64*
air conditioner **erkon** [3–13] *14*
air pollution **polusyon sa hangin** [14–37] *37*
air quality **kalidad ng hangin** [28–23] *65*
airplane **eroplano** [12–4] *32*
airport **paliparan; erport** [11–2] *30*; [31–36] *71*
alarm clock **orasang may alarm** [15–12] *38*
algebra **alhebra** [19–38] *47*
All Saints' Day **Araw ng mga Santo** [18–5] *44*
All Souls' Day **Araw ng mga Patay** [18–6] *44*
almost **halos; muntik na** [34–40] *77*
alphabet **alpabeto** [20–21] *49*
already **na** [13–59] *35*
also **rin; din** [20–43] *49*; [34–38] *77*
although **bagamat** [28–39] *65*
altogether **lahat** [10–32] *29*
always **palagi** [25–37] *59*
ambulance **ambulansya** [27–21] *63*
America **Amerika** [32–5] *72*
an octagon **oktagon; waluhang-sulok** [7–20] *23*
an oval **obalo; hugis-itlog** [7–24] *23*

Android phones **teleponong Android** [24–7] *56*
ankle **bukung-bukong** [4–29] *17*
anniversary **anibersaryo** [18–32] *45*
another **sa iba** [31–45] *71*
Antartica **Antartika** [32–18] *72*
antiseptic **antiseptiko** [27–36] *63*
anxious; worried **nag-aalala** [27–45] *63*
apartment **paupahan** [3–52] *14*
apartment; house **apartment; bahay** [3–51] *14*; [11–25] *31*
apartment building **apartment** [11–13] *30*
apple (fruit) **mansanas** [36–37] *82*
Apple **Apple** [24–22] *57*
Apple phones (iPhones) **teleponong Apple** [24–8] *56*
application (computer program) **aplikeysyon** [23–46] *55*
appointment **iskedyul** [27–20] *63*
apprentice **baguhan** [25–27] *59*
April **Abril** [16–19] *41*
Arabic **Arabe** [33–9] *74*
archipelago **kapuluan** [38–3] *86*
architect **arkitekto** [25–9] *58*
area; side **bandá** [22–12] *53*
arm **braso** [4–19] *17*
arrive **dumating** [8–20] *25*
art museum **museong pansining** [11–14] *31*
artery **arterya** [4–45] *17*
artist **alagad ng sining** [25–7] *58*
artist; actor; actress **artista; aktor; aktres** [26–32] *61*
as a result of **bilang resulta; kaya** [28–40] *65*
Asia **Asya** [32–16] *72*
asking directions **pagtatanong ng direksyon** [13–16] *34*
assignment **takdang aralin** [19–32] *47*; [21–41] *51*
attend a birthday party **dumalo sa salo-salo para sa kaarawan** [18–28] *45*
attic; loft **silid sa itaas ng bahay; kuwarto sa itaas ng bahay** [3–54] *14*
audience **manonood** [26–14] *61*
auditorium **awditoryum** [20–18] *49*
August **Agosto** [16–23] *41*
aunt (mother's sister) **tita** [2–17] *13*
Australia **Australya** [32–17] *72*
autumn; fall **taglagas** [17–3] *42*

B

bad **masama** [8–7] *24*
bad weather **masamang panahon** [14–35] *37*
badminton **badminton** [30–5] *68*
baked coconut rice cake **bibingka** [35–3] *78*
balcony **balkonahe** [3–2] *14*
ball **bola** [30–27] *69*
banana **saging** [36–43] *82*
band **bánda** [22–12] *53*; [26–27] *61*
bandage **bendahe** [27–54] *63*
bandurria **bandurya** [26–7] *60*
bank **bangko** [11–7] *30*
bank deposit **deposito sa bangko** [9–33] *27*
banquet; reception **salusalo** [18–34] *45*
baseball **beysbol** [30–7] *68*
basement; cellar **silid sa ibaba ng bahay; kuwarto sa ibaba ng bahay; silong** [3–55] *14*
bat **paniki** [38–18] *87*
bathroom **liguan** [3–37] *15*
bathtub **banyera** [3–42] *15*

bazaar **tiangge** [10–21] *29*
beach **tabing-dagat; dalampasigan** [31–33] *71*; [39–8] *88*
beach wave **alon** [39–28] *89*
bean sprouts **toge** [37–14] *84*
beans **bins** [36–73] *83*
bear **oso** [29–6] *66*
beef **karneng baka** [37–2] *84*
because **dahil** [23–52] *55*
because of **dahil sa** [28–31] *65*
bed **kama** [3–20] *14*
bedroom **kuwarto; silidtulugan** [3–21] *14*
bee **bubuyog** [29–26] *67*
beer **serbesa** [36–23] *81*
before **bago** [15–28] *39*; **dati** [17–19] *43*; begin **simula** [8–23] *25*
behind **sa likod** [13–15] *34*
bell pepper **siling pimiento** [37–23] *85*
below **sa ilalim** [13–5] *34*
belt **sinturon** [10–19] *29*
between; among **pagitan** [15–29] *39*
beverage **mga inumin** [36–1] *80*
bicycle **bisikleta** [30–11] *68*
big **malaki** [8–11] *25*
bill; invoice **bil; kuwenta** [10–40] *29*
biology **biyolohiya** [19–41] *47*
bird **ibon** [29–20] *67*
birthday **kaarawan** [18–27] *45*
bitter gourd **ampalaya** [37–38] *85*
black **itim** [7–4] *22*
blackboard **blakbord; itim na pisara** [20–2] *48*
blouse **blusa** [10–7] *28*
blood **dugo** [4–42] *17*
blood pressure **presyon sa dugo** [27–9] *62*
blood test **suriin ang dugo** [27–7] *62*
blue **asul** [7–6] *22*
boarding pass **bording pas** [31–9] *70*
boiled **nilaga** [35–30] *79*
boiled duck-egg embryo **balut** [35–2] *78*
bone **buto** [4–44] *17*
bonfire **siga** [38–14] *87*
book **libro** [19–7] *46*
book shelf **lagayan ng mga libro** [3–35] *15*
boots **bota** [14–3] *36*
borrow **hiramin** [8–29] *25*
bottle **bote** [36–30] *81*
bottle gourd **úpo** [22–2] *52*; [37–46] *85*
boutique **maliit na tindahan** [10–24] *29*
bowl **mangkok** [34–13] *76*
brain **utak** [4–30] *17*
bread **tinapay** [34–8] *76*
breakfast **agahan** [34–31] *77*
bridge **tulay** [11–26] *31*
broccoli **brokoli** [37–33] *85*
brother-in-law **bayaw** [2–36] *12*
brothers **magkapatid na lalaki** [2–12] *13*
brown **kulay tsokolate** [7–9] *22*
bruise **pasá** [22–16] *53*
budget inn **murang tuluyan** [31–26] *71*
bus route **ruta ng bus** [12–34] *33*
bus stop **sakayan ng bus** [12–13] *33*
busy **abala** [8–8] *24*
but; however **pero** [28–36] *65*
butterfly **paruparo** [29–27] *67*
by **gamit ang** [28–30] *65*

C

CD; DVD **CD; dibidi** [23–12] *54*
cabbage **repolyo** [37–43] *85*
cabinet **kabinet** [3–25] *15*; **gabinete** [32–53] *73*
cable **kable** [24–34] *56*

cake **keyk** [35–17] *79*
calculator **kalkyuleytor** [5-16] *19*; [20–11] *48*
calculus **kalkulus** [19–42] *47*
calendar **kalendaryo** [16–1] *40*
camera **kamera** [31–15] *70*
cantaloupe **milong bilog** [36–53] *82*
cape **kápa** [22–9] *53*
car **kotse** [12–1] *32*
caramel custard **letse flan** [35–21] *79*
caramelized sugar **arnibal** [35–34] *79*
carpet **karpet; alpombra** [3–12] *14*
carrot **karot** [37–34] *85*
cashew nuts **kasuy** [36–66] *83*
cash **cash** [9–38] *27*
cashier **kahera** [10–26] *29*
cat **pusa** [29–22] *67*
catch a bus **habulin ang biyahe ng bus** [12-23] *33*
catch a train **habulin ang biyahe ng tren** [12-24] *33*
cauliflower **koliplor** [37–44] *85*
cave **kuweba** [38–8] *86*
ceiling **kisame** [3-4] *14*
celery **seleri** [37–28] *85*
cello **tselo** [26–16] *61*
certainly **walang duda** [10–33] *29*
cent **sentimo** [9-3] *26*
central business district (CBD) **sentral na distrito ng negosyo** [11-23] *31*
century (100 years) **siglo** [16–38] *41*
chair **upuan** [3-8] *14*
Champagne **syampeyn** [36–21] *81*
changes **pagbabago** [28–28] *65*
charger **charger** [24–35] *56*
cheap **mura** [9–28] *27*
check **tseke** [9–19] *27*
cheek **pisngi** [4-4] *16*
cheese **keso** [35–18] *79*
chef **punong tagapagluto** [25–11] *59*
chemistry **kemistri** [19–40] *47*
chest **dibdib** [4–26] *17*
chestnuts **kastanyas** [36–65] *83*
chicken **manok** [29–19] *67*; [37–6] *84*
chicken barbecue **barbekyung manok** [35–23] *79*
chicken ginger stew **tinola** [34–9] *76*
children **mga bata** [2-3] *12*
chili peppers **sili** [37–36] *85*
chin **baba** [4–13] *16*; **bába** [22–1] *52*
China **Tsina** [32–3] *72*
Chinese cabbage **pechay Baguio** [37–16] *84*
Chinese New Year's Cake **tikoy** [18–11] *44*
chocolates **mga tsokolate** [18–16] *45*
choice **píli** [22–15] *53*; **pili** [34–36] *77*
chopsticks **tsapstiks** [34–12] *76*
chosen **pilí** [22–15] *53*
Christmas **Pasko** [18–25] *45*
church **simbahan** [11–33] *31*
cinema **sinehan** [11-20] *31*
city **lungsod; siyudad** [11-11] *30*; [32–71] *73*
clams **kabibe** [39–13] *88*
classical music **musikang klasikal** [26–26] *61*
classmates **kaklase** [20–13] *48*
classroom **silid-aralan; klasrum** [20–4] *48*
clean **malinis** [28–17] *65*
clean energy **malinis na enerhiya** [28–20] *65*
clear (sky) **maaliwalas** [14-4] *36*
clear day **maaliwalas na araw** [14–5] *36*
clock **orasan** [15–6] *38*
closed **sarado** [8–12] *25*
clothes **mga damit** [10–6] *28*

clothing size laki ng kasuotan [7–29] 23

clouds mga ulap [14–24] 37

cloudy day makulimlim [14–7] 36

coal uling [28–22] 65

coat or jacket jaket [14–18] 37

cocktails kakteyl [36–17] 81

coconut niyog [36–42] 82

coconut flower wine tuba [36–32] 81

coconut oil langis ng niyog [37–62] 85

coconut vodka lambanog [36–33] 81

coffee mga inumin [36–6] 80

coffee kape [3–11] 14

coins barya [9-2] 26

cola kok [36–9] 80

cold malamig [14–22] 37

cold dish (appetizer) malamig na pampagana [34–21] 77

cold water malamig na tubig [36–26] 81

cold weather malamig na panahon [14–23] 37

cold weather clothes damit panlamig [14–39] 37

colleague kasama sa trabaho; katrabaho [25–24] 59

college kolehiyo [20–34] 49

colors mga kulay [7–1] 22

come pumunta [8–17] 25

comma kuwit [21–16] 51

company kumpanya [25-20] 59

comparing prices pagkukumpara ng presyo [10–28] 29

competition paligsahan [30–13] 69

complete kumpleto [28–33] 65

comprehension pag-unawa [21–57] 51

computer lab kompyuter lab [20–19] 49

computers mga kompyuter [23–1] 54

concert konsiyerto [26–13] 61

conference center lugar ng kumperensiya [11–8] 30

conscientious; serious masipag; seryoso [19–46] 47

cook; chef tagaluto [34–3] 76

cooked rice kanin [34–14] 76

cooking oil mantika [37–60] 85

coral koral [39–13] 88

correct tama [21–42] 51

corn mais [36–84] 83

corruption korupsyon [32–82] 73

cosmetics pampaganda [10–17] 29

Councilor Konsehal [32–67] 73

Countries in Southeast Asia Mga bansa sa Timog-Siliangan Asya [32–17] 72

country bansa [32–68] 73

course; academic program kurso; programang pang-akademiko [21–40] 51

cousins mga pinsan [2-24] 13

cow baká [22–20] 53; [29–13] 67

crab alimango [39–11] 88

crackers galyetas [36–80] 83

credit card kredit kard [9–21] 27; [10–30] 29

crocodile buwaya [39–7] 88

crops pananim [17–17] 43

cruise center sentro ng paglalayag [31–37] 71

cucumber pipino [37–32] 85

culture kultura [21–35] 51

currency pera [31–21] 71

currency exchange palitan ng pera [9–23] 27

curry powder pulbos ng kari [37–58] 85

curtain kurtina [3-17] 14

custard apple atis [36–45] 82

customs kostoms [31–27] 71

cute; adorable kyut; kahanga-hanga [29–31] 67

D

dance (performance art) sumayaw [26–20] 61

dangerous mapanganib [38-34] 87

dark color madilim na kulay [7–15] 22

daughter anak na babae [2-4] 12

day araw [16–3] 40

day of a month araw sa isang buwan [16–36] 41

decade (10 years) dekada [16–37] 41

December Disyembre [16–27] 41

debt utang [9–32] 27

decision desisyon; pasiya [10–36] 29

deep fried pork leg krispy pata [34–43] 77

deep fried sweet rice balls covered in sesame seeds butsi-butsi [35–14] 79

deep-fried pork skin with salt tsitsaron [35–42] 79

delivery van tagahatid na van [12–7] 32

demeanor dating [22–17] 53

dentist dentista [25-14] 59

dentistry pagdedentista [27–23] 63

depart umalis [8-20] 25

department kagawaran [32–54] 73

department store tindahan sa mall [10–23] 29

dermatology dermatolohiya [27–29] 63

desk lamesa [3-36] 15

desktop computer kompyuter desktop [23–4] 54

dessert panghimagas [35–38] 79

diary talaarawan [16–44] 41

dictionary diksiyunaryo [19–11] 46

diet drinks inuming pandiyeta [36–10] 80

difficult mahirap [8–15] 25; [21–12] 50

digestive system sistemang dihestibo [4-37] 17

digits mga numero [5-29] 19

dimsum siomai [34–6] 76

dinner hapunan [34–33] 77

dinosaur dinosawro [29–10] 66

direction direksyon [13-36] 35

discount diskuwento [9–27] 27

distance layo [13-37] 35

do not have wala [8-16] 25

doctor doktor [27–4] 62

doctor's consultation room silid-konsultasyon ng doktor [27–18] 62

dog aso [29–21] 67

dollar dolyar [9-9] 26

door pintuan [3-46] 15

down baba [8-1] 24

downstairs babâ [22–1] 52

downtown bayan; sentro [11-22] 31

drawer drower [3-34] 15

dried fruits pinatuyong prutas [36–82] 83

dried meat tapa [34–45] 77

drive a car magmaneho ng kotse [12-26] 33

driver drayber [12-3] 32

drums tambol [26–6] 60

duck pato [37–5] 84

duck egg penoy [35–25] 79

E

eagle agila [38-19] 87

ear tenga [4-2] 16

ear, nose, and throat tenga, ilong at lalamunan [27–25] 63

earphones earphones [26–25] 61

early maaga [15–24] 39

early morning madaling araw [15–18] 39

earth; ground lupa [28–29] 65

east silangan [13-10] 34

Easter Araw ng Pagkabuhay [18–20] 45

easy madali [8-15] 25; [21–11] 50

easy to use madaling gamitin [23–37] 55

easy-to-eat mabilis kainin [35–40] 79

economics ekonomika [19–37] 47

eggplant talong [37–26] 85

eggs itlog [37–39] 85

eight walo [5-8] 18

elbow siko [4-20] 17

election eleksyon [32–76] 73

electric car kotseng de-kuryente [28–6] 64

electric socket; power point saksakan [3-50] 14

elementary school eskuwelahang pang-elementarya [20–30] 49

elephant elepante [29–14] 67

elevator elebeytor [3-45] 15

email i-meyl [23–15] 54

emergency emerhensya [27–39] 63

emergency room kuwartong pang-emerdyensi [27–2] 62

employee empleyado [25–26] 59

end katapusan [8-23] 25

energy drinks inuming nagbibigay-enerhiya [36–15] 80

engineer inhinyero [25–4] 58

English Ingles [33–1] 74

enter pasukan [8-6] 24

enthusiastic masigasig [2-43] 12

entrepreneur negosyante [25–21] 59

environment kalikasan [28–26] 65

equals sumatotal; kalalabasan [5-21] 19

eraser pambura [19–14] 47

essay sanaysay [21–33] 51

Europe Europa [32–15] 72

even more mas marami [10–35] 29

even numbers numerong even [5-25] 19

exams eksamen [19–1] 46

exclamation mark tandang padamdam [21–13] 51

exercise book aklat sa pag sasanay [21–3] 50

exit labasan [8-6] 24

expensive mahal [9–29] 27

expressway ekspreswey [11-18] 31

eye mata [4-8] 16

eyebrow kilay [4-7] 16

F

face mukha [4-5] 16

Facebook Facebook [24–18] 57

fake peke [8–26] 25

falls talon [39–4] 88

family pamilya [2-40] 12

famous sikát [22–18] 53; [26–30] 61

fan pamaypay [17–14] 43

far malayo [8–24] 25; [13–43] 35

farmer magsasaka [25–19] 59

fast mabilis [8–27] 25

fast to upload mabilis mag-upload [23–36] 55

fat mataba [8–13] 25

Father's Day Araw ng mga Tatay [18–12] 44

father's elder brother nakatatandang kapatid ng tatay [2-11] 13

father's sister kapatid na babae ng tatay; tita [2-29] 12

father's younger brother nakababatang kapatid na lalaki ng tatay; tito [2-28] 12

Feast of the Nazarene Pista ng Nazareno [18–23] 45

February Pebrero [16–17] 41

female babae [2-3] 12

festival; holiday pista; pagdiriwang [18–1] 44

fever lagnat [27–12] 62

fifteen minutes past six kinse minutos pasado alas-sais [15–8] 38

fifteen minutes to seven kinse minutos bago mag-alas-siyete [15–10] 38

file payl [23–43] 55

Filipino dish made of chopped deep fried pork head skin and liver sisig [34–23] 77

Filipino language wikang Filipino [21–17] 51

Filipino restaurant restawrang Filipino [34–1] 76

Filipino sausage longganisa [34–42] 77

Filipino spring roll made with vegetables lumpia [34–10] 76

finally sa wakas [15–36] 39

financier tagapondo [25–3] 58

fingers mga daliri [4-15] 17

finish line katapusan ng linya [30–14] 69

fire engine pamatay-sunog na trak [12-16] 33

firefighter bumbero [25–18] 59

fireworks paputok [18–3] 44

first aid kit kit para sa pangunang lunas [27–53] 63

fish isda [29–28] 67; [37–8] 84; [39–16] 88

fish meat sausage kikiyam [35–7] 78

fish sauce patis [37–54] 85

five lima [5-5] 18

five minutes past six singko minutos pasado alas-sais [15–5] 38

five minutes to seven singko minutos bago mag-alas-siyete [15–11] 38

floor sahig [3-16] 14

flour arina [36–85] 83

flower bulaklak [17–7] 42; [28–2] 64

Flower Festival Pista ng Panagbenga [18–22] 45

flute plauta [26–10] 60

fog hamog [14–25] 37

foot paa [4-23] 17; talampakan [13-41] 35

for the purpose of para sa [28–32] 65

forehead noo [4-17] 17

forest gubat [28–13] 65; [38–4] 86

forest fire sunog sa gubat [38-18] 87

forgotten nakalimutan [8–30] 25

fork tinidor [34–17] 76

former dáting [22–17] 53

four apat [5-4] 18

four seasons apat na panahon [17–18] 43

fraction maliit na bahagi; praksyon [5-24] 19

free wifi libreng wifi [31–31] 71

French Pranses [33–2] 74

frequently madalas [15–33] 39

fresh sariwa [37–50] 85

fresh soft tofu with sweetener, and sago pearl taho [35–9] 78

freshman year in college unang taon sa kolehiyo [20–35] 49

freshwater sariwang tubig [39–27] 89

Friday Biyernes [16–14] 40

fried pinirito [35–29] 79

fried banana rolls in caramelized sugar turon [35–27] 79

fried rice sinangag [34–7] 76

fried-sugared banana bananakyu [35–6] 78

friend kaibígan [22–10] 53

friends mga kaibigan [1-13] 10

from mula [27–43] 63

fruit juice katas ng prutas [36–3] 80

full busog [8–19] 25; punô [22–4] 52

fun sayá [22–14] 53

future hinaharap [8–22] 25

G

garage garahe [3-56] 14

garbage truck trak ng basura [12-6] 32

garden hardin [28–1] 64

garlic bawang [37–25] 85

gas station; petrol station istasyon ng gas [11–6] 30

gathering; meeting pagtitipon; pulonga [1-19] 11

general medicine pangkalahatang medisina [27–23] 63

general surgery pangkalahatang operasyon [27–24] 63

generally sa pangkalahatan [10–34] 29

geography heyograpiya [19–43] 47

geometry heyometriya [19–34] 47

German Aleman [33–4] 74

Germany Alemanya [32–6] 72

get internet service at home home magpakabit ng internet sa bahay

right side sa kanang bahagi [13-27] *35*
river ilog [28–8] *64*; [39–1] *88*
Rizal Day Araw ni Rizal [18–14] *44*
road kalye [11-29] *31*
roasted suckling pig lechon [34–11] *76*
rocky mabato [34-29] *87*
roof bubong [3-53] *14*
room kuwarto [3-22] *14*
root ugat [38–6] *86*
roses mga rosas [18–17] *45*
rowing pagsasagwan [30–18] *69*
rugby ragbi [30–3] *68*
ruler panukat [19–17] *47*
rules patakaran [32–72] *73*
running pagtakbo [30–9] *68*
Russia Rusiya [32–9] *72*
Russian Ruso [33–3] *74*

S

S size maliit na sukat [7-31] *23*
sad malungkot [8-31] *25*
salt asin [37–56] *85*
same; identical pareho; magkatulad [29–34] *67*
sand buhangin [39–29] *89*
Santa Claus Santa Klaws [18–26] *45*
satisfied kontento [1-9] *10*
Saturday Sabado [16–15] *40*
savings ipon [9–22] *27*
scarf bandana [10–20] *29*
scallions; spring onions dahon ng sibuyas [37–22] *85*
school paaralan; eskwelahan [20–16] *48*
school holidays mga araw na walang pasok sa eskuwela [18–31] *45*
school is over wala nang pasok [6–26] *20*
science agham [19–35] *47*; [20–12] *48*
scissors gunting [19–21] *47*
screen iskrin [23–2] *54*
sea dagat [39–25] *89*
seafood pagkaing-dagat [37–7] *84*
seasonings pampalasa; rekado [37–51] *85*
seawater tubig–dagat [39–26] *89*
second segundo [15–3] *38*
secretary kalihim [25–17] *58*
self sarili [2-41] *12*
selfie selfie; kunan ang sarili [24–1] *57*
Senator Senador [32–56] *73*
senior high school senior hayskul [20–32] *49*
senior year in college huling taon sa kolehiyo [20–38] *49*
sentence pangungusap [21-31] *51*
September Setyembre [16–24] *41*
serenade harana [26–15] *61*
service provider tagabigay ng serbisyo [25-33] *59*
sesame seeds linga [36–72] *83*
seven pito [5-7] *18*; pitó [22–7] *52*
Seven continents of the world Pitong kontinente ng mundo [32–11] *72*
several times makailang beses [27–44] *63*
shake hands magkamayan [1-28] *11*
shape hugis [7-39] *23*
shark pating [39–6] *88*
shaved ice with corn kernel mais kon yelo [35–32] *79*
shaved ice with milk and mixed fruits and beans halo-halo [35–12] *78*
sheep tupa [29–12] *67*
shift work oras ng trabaho [25-29] *59*
shine síkat [22–18] *53*
shirt polo [10–14] *28*
shoes sapatos [10–13] *28*
shoot! tirá! [22–6] *52*
shop tindahan [10–22] *29*; [11–3] *30*
shop staff tindera sa tindahan [10–25] *29*
Shopee Shopee [24–20] *57*
shopping bag lalagyan ng pinamili [10–4] *28*

shopping center; mall pamilihan; mall [11–17] *31*
short pandak [8-5] *24*; maikli [8-9] *24*
shoulder balikat [4-24] *17*
shovel pála [22–13] *53*
shower paliguan; syawer [3-41] *15*
shrimp; prawns hipon; sugpo [37–10] *84*; [39–12] *88*
shrimp paste bagoong [37–55] *85*
side bahagi [13–49] *35*
sidewalk bangketa [11–27] *31*
sightseeing pagliliwaliw [31–28] *71*
silver pilak [7-14] *22*
simmered oxtail and vegetables in peanut-based sauce kare-kare [34–20] *77*
Singles' Day Araw para sa mga nag-iisa [18–33] *45*
singer mang-aawit [26–28] *61*
sink lababo [3-40] *15*
sister-in-law hipag [2-37] *12*
sisters magkapatid na babae [2-16] *13*
sit upô [22–2] *52*
six anim [5-6] *18*
size sukat [7-39] *23*
skeletal system sistemang skeletal [4-40] *17*
skin balat [4-41] *17*
skin burn páso [22–8] *52*
skinny payat [8-13] *25*
ship; boat barko; bangka [12-14] *33*
short story maikling kuwento [21–54] *51*
SIM card SIM kard [24–30] *56*
skiing pag-iski [30–17] *69*
skirt palda [10–8] *28*
skyscraper napakataas na gusali [11–12] *30*
slippers tsinelas [39–21] *89*
slippery madulas [38-30] *87*
slow mabagal [8-27] *25*
slow down bagalan [12-28] *33*
slow internet connection mabagal ang koneksyon ng internet [23–35] *55*
slow-cook matagal maluto [35–41] *79*
small maliit [7-37] *23*; [8-11] *25*
small change barya [9–20] *27*
small horizontally laid gongs kulintang [26–2] *60*
smaller mas maliit [7-41] *23*
smartphone smartphone [24–1] *56*
smartwatch smartwatch [15–14] *39*
smile ngiti [1-31] *11*
snack meryenda [35–37] *79*
snake ahas [29–17] *67*
snow niyebe [14–15] *36*
snowball fights batuhan ng bola ng niyebe [17–15] *43*
social studies araling panlipunan [19–36] *47*
socks medyas [10–12] *28*
sodas sopdrinks [36–24] *81*
sofa sopa [3-15] *14*
solar energy enerhiyang mula sa araw [28–9] *64*
son anak na lalake [2-1] *12*
son/daughter-in-law manugang [2-31] *12*
song kanta [21–53] *51*
sophomore year in college pangalawang taon sa kolehiyo [20–36] *49*
sound tunog [6-18] *20*
soup sabaw [34–34] *77*
sour soup made with pork ribs and vegetables sinigang na baboy [34–27] *77*
south timog [13-13] *34*
South America Timog Amerika [32–13] *72*
southeast timog silangan [13-12] *34*
southwest timog kanluran [13-11] *34*
souvenir shop bilihan ng pasalubong [31–14] *70*
soy milk soya [36–4] *80*
soy sauce toyo [37–52] *85*
Spanish Espanyol [33–6] *74*
Spanish plums siniguwelas [36–61] *82*

speak magsalita [21–51] *51*
special espesyal [34–37] *77*
spinach espinaka [37–17] *84*
sponge gourd patola [37–21] *84*
spoon kutsara [34–19] *76*
sports car kotseng pangisports [12–10] *32*
sports drinks inuming pang-isports [36–16] *80*
sports shirt; sweatshirt polong pang-isports [30–25] *69*
sports shoes; sneakers sapatos na pang-isports [30–26] *69*
spring tagsibol [17–1] *42*; bukal [39–5] *88*
Spring Festival (Chinese New Year) Bagong Taon ng mga Tsino [18–7] *44*
sprint mabilisang takbuhan [30–8] *68*
squid pusit [37–9] *84*; [39–17] *88*
stand up tayô [22–11] *53*
star apple kaymito [36–58] *82*
starch arina [37–58] *85*
stadium istadyum [11–15] *31*
steamed bun siopao [34–22] *77*
steamed fish pinasingawang isda [34–26] *77*
steamed sweet rice cake puto [35–13] *78*
stomach tiyan [4-49] *17*
stopwatch segundometro [15–13] *38*
story kuwento [19–31] *47*
stove kalan; lutuan [3-31] *15*
strawberry presa [36–51] *82*
street kalye [11–4] *30*
street corner kanto [11–31] *31*
strong signal malakas ang signal [24–12] *57*
student estudyante [20–15] *48*
study room silid-aralan [3-32] *15*
study time oras ng pag-aaral [6-35] *20*
string bean sitaw [37–15] *84*
strange hindi karaniwan [29–38] *67*
suburb labas ng lungsod [11–24] *31*
sudden bigla [15–35] *39*
sugar cane tubò [22–19] *53*
suitcase maleta [31–5] *70*
summer tag-araw [17–2] *42*
summer vacation bakasyon para sa tag-araw [18–29] *45*
summit tuktok [38-28] *87*
sun araw [14–26] *37*
Sunday Linggo [16–5] *40*; [16–9] *40*
sunny weather maaraw [14–36] *37*
surname apelyido [1-24] *11*
subway daan sa ilalim ng lupa [12-11] *33*
sun shade lilim [17–10] *42*
sunblock lotion pamahid na panlaban sa araw [17–16] *43*
supermarket groseri [11–5] *30*
(surprise marker) palá [22–13] *53*
sweater sweter [14–19] *37*
sweet chocolate rice porridge champorado [34–29] *77*
sweet cured pork belly tocino [34–41] *77*
sweet potato with caramelized sugar in sticks kamotekyu [35–26] *79*
sweet rice cake covered in coconut, sugar and sesame palitaw [35–31] *79*
sweet sticky rice biko [35–8] *78*
swimming paglangoy [30–19] *69*

T

table lamesa [3-14] *14*
table tennis pingpong [30–1] *68*
tablet tablet [23–3] *54*
table lamp lampara para sa mesa [3-33] *15*
Tagalog Tagalog [33–17] *75*
Tagalog-English mix Taglish [21–18] *51*
take a bus; by bus sumakay ng bus [12-22] *33*
Take care! Ingat! [1-18] *11*
take off hubarin [8-14] *25*
talent; ability talento; kakayahan [19–45] *47*
tall matangkad [8-5] *24*

tangerine dalanghita [36–40] *82*
tap water tubig mula sa gripo [36–11] *80*
tapioca pearl sago [35–10] *78*
tariff taripa [32–81] *73*
tax buwis [9–37] *27*; [32–80] *73*
tax free walang buwisa [10–41] *29*
taxi taksi [12–2] *32*
tea tsaa [36–7] *80*
teacher guro; titser [20–6] *48*
teeth ngipin [4-12] *16*
telephone operator opereytor ng telepono [25-10] *58*
television telebisyon [3-10] *14*
temple templo [11-37] *31*
ten sampu [5-10] *18*
tennis tenis [30–22] *69*
test pagsusulit [19–44] *47*
textbook teksbuk [20–26] *49*
texting pagteteks [24–24] *56*
Thai Tay [33–15] *75*
Thank you! Salamat [1-21] *11*
Thanksgiving Araw ng Pasasalamat [18–18] *45*
the East sa Silangan [13–45] *35*
the North sa Hilaga [13–48] *35*
the news ang balita [19–8] *46*
the same as kapareho ng [10–31] *29*
the South sa Timog [13–46] *35*
the West sa Kanluran [13–47] *35*
the year after next taon matapos ang susunod na taon [16–32] *41*
the year before noong isang taon [16–29] *41*
there doon [13–3] *34*
they sila [21–10] *50*
thigh hita [4-28] *17*
things mga gamit [10–39] *29*
thirsty uhaw [36–14] *80*
this year ngayong taon [16–30] *41*
three tatlo [5-3] *18*
three quarters tatlong kapat [5-12] *18*
thunder kulog [14–13] *36*
thunderstorm ulan at pagkulog [14–14] *36*
Thursday Huwebes [16–13] *40*
ticket counter bilihan ng tiket [12-33] *33*
tiger tigre [29–4] *66*
time oras [15–17] *39*
tired; worn out pagod [27–41] *63*
to be allergic; allergy may alerji sa [36–86] *83*
to accomplish matapos [28–34] *65*
to add dagdagan [5-20] *19*
to affect maapektuhan [28–35] *65*
to agree sumang-ayon [6-43] *20*
to allow payagan [13–58] *35*
to answer sumagot [6-22] *20*; [19–6] *46*
to appear magpakita [29–36] *67*
to appreciate; to enjoy magustuhan [26–18] *61*
to ask magtanong [6-19] *20*
to attend elementary school pumasok sa elementarya [20–29] *49*
to bathe maligo [3-48] *15*
to be afraid matakot [29–30] *67*
to be concerned about mag-alala tungkol sa; kay [27–48] *63*
to be lost mawala [13-35] *35*
to be willing (to do something) magkusa [6-42] *20*
to become aware of maging mapag-matiyag; maging malay sa [31–44] *71*
to believe maniwala [2-44] *12*
to bow yumuko [1-33] *11*
to breathe huminga [6-21] *20*
to bring magdala [10–38] *29*
to brush teeth magsipilyo [6-11] *21*
to buy bumili [10–1] *28*
to call on the phone tawagan [1-12] *10*
to call; to be called tawagin [1-12] *10*
to call a taxi tumawag ng taksi [12-36] *33*

Published by Tuttle Publishing, an imprint of Periplus Editions (HK) Ltd

www.tuttlepublishing.com

ISBN: 978-0-8048-3915-0

23 22 21   10 9 8 7 6 5 4 3
Printed in Malaysia   2105TO

"Books to Span the East and West"

Tuttle Publishing was founded in 1832 in the small New England town of Rutland, Vermont [USA]. Our core values remain as strong today as they were then-to publish best-in-class books which bring people together one page at a time. In 1948, we established a publishing office in Japan–and Tuttle is now a leader in publishing English-language books about the arts, languages and cultures of Asia. The world has become a much smaller place today and Asia's economic and cultural influence has grown. Yet the need for meaningful dialogue and information about this diverse region has never been greater. Over the past seven decades, Tuttle has published thousands of books on subjects ranging from martial arts and paper crafts to language learning and literature–and our talented authors, illustrators, designers and photographers have won many prestigious awards. We welcome you to explore the wealth of information available on Asia at **www.tuttlepublishing.com.**

Distributed by

North America, Latin America & Europe
Tuttle Publishing
364 Innovation Drive
North Clarendon,
VT 05759-9436 U.S.A.
Tel: 1 (802) 773-8930
Fax: 1 (802) 773-6993
info@tuttlepublishing.com
www.tuttlepublishing.com

Japan
Tuttle Publishing
Yaekari Building, 3rd Floor
5-4-12 Osaki
Shinagawa-ku
Tokyo 141-0032
Tel: (81) 3 5437-0171
Fax: (81) 3 5437-0755
sales@tuttle.co.jp
www.tuttle.co.jp

Asia Pacific
Berkeley Books Pte. Ltd.
3 Kallang Sector #04-01/02
Singapore 349278
Tel: (65) 6741-2178
Fax: (65) 6741-2179
inquiries@periplus.com.sg
www.tuttlepublishing.com

The Online Audio files for pronunciation practice may be Downloaded.

To download the audios for this book, type the URL below into your web browser.

https://www.tuttlepublishing.com/Tagalog-Picture-Dictionary

For support, email us at info@tuttlepublishing.com

Photo Credits

123rf.com: lightfieldstudios 53; / **Bigstockphoto.com:** tonyoquias 26; / **Dreamstime.com:** Adeliepenguin 52; Alexander Mychko 76, 77; Alexander Potapov 86; Alphaspirit 52; Anat Chantrakool 82; Andrew Deer 87; Anna Rutkovskaya 52; Anthony James 79; Antonio Oquias 44, 45; Appfind 78; Barna Tanko 78; Belier 78; Bluestrat1 76; Bluetoes67 52; Brian Siegelwax 78; Bruno Ismael Da Silva Alves 87; Buppha Wuttifery 82; Chireau 53; Draftmode 82; Draghicich 87; Edwardgerges 52; Edwin Verin 87; Evgenyatamanenko 52; Geerati 87; Georgi1969 50; Georgerudy 62; Goytex 79; Grey 79; Hannahpazdeleon 86; Harold Bonacquist *covers*, 33; Hrlumanog 44; Inara Prusakova 52; Jamesteohart 53; Jennifer Pitiquen 44; Jianghongyan 84; Jitthiluk Rachomas 82; Jonald John Morales 86; Jose Gil *covers*, 60; Jovani Carlo Gorospe 61; Juliengrondin 52; Junpinzon 78; Just2shutter 84; Korradol 84; Kristel Cuadra 79; Lance Bellers 52; Li Lin 37; Lucy Brown 87; Lukas Gojda 79; Lumen Bilat 45; Maksershov 86; Merlyn Cahalim 86; Michael Manzano 44; Mohamed Ahmed Soliman 57; Mr.smith Chetanachan 84; Naropano 86; Natalya Aksenova 67; Natcha Insiripong 85; Namhwi Kim 76; Oleg Dudko 87; Oleksandr Shyripa 86; Olga Khoroshunova 86; Olyina 82; Omgeijutsuka 78; Oscar Calero 52; Paulus Rusyanto 50; Phuongphoto *covers*, 26, 33, 44; Ppy2010ha 3, 77; Rafael Ben Ari 53; Rawpixelimages 52; Recyap8 *covers*, 77, 78, 79; Robhainer 52; Robin Nieuwenkamp 86; Ruby B. Llamas *covers*, 76; Ruslanchik 78; Sanse293 *covers*, 60; Sarayuth Punnasuriyaporn 52; Savin Sorin Matei Contescu 52; Seanjeeves 76, 77, 78; Shariff Che\' Lah 84; Shevs 87; Simon Gurney 86; Stephen Mcsweeny 87; Suthisa Kaewkajang 82; Tawat Hantrakool 84; Tmyra 26; Valentyn75 87; Viacheslav Dubrovin 78; Vince Sambo 77; Vishakha Shah 52; Willeecole 87; Xpdream 52; Yooran Park *covers*, 78; / **Shuttlestock.com:** 06photo 76; 89studio 47; AboutLife 2, 59; Africa Studio 24, 29, 39, 48, 60, 80, 84; aijiro 77; akepong srichaichana 83; Aleksandar Todorovic 72; AlenKadr 76; Aleks_Shutter 45; Alex Staroseltsev 67; Alexander Raths 74; ALEXEY FILATOV 54; AlexLMX 46; Alhovik 23; All kind of people 41; amasterphotographer 82; AmyLv 83; Andrey Burmakin 70; Andrey_Popov 11, 21, 58; angelo lano 42; Annette Shaff 16; Anton_Ivanov 31; antpkr 24; Anucha Naisuntorn 38; Apple's Eyes Studio 62; arek_malang 21; Art_Photo 10; Artem_Graf 81; artemisphoto 45; ArtFamily 35; ArtOfPhotos 34; ARTYOORAN 30; ARZTSAMUI 28; Ase 64; asiandelight 43; Asier Romero 10, 20; aslysun 15, 16, 20, 21, 62; Athapet Piruksa 54; Atstock Productions 63; AVAVA 58; AYakovlev *covers*, 60; azure1 83; BalancePhoto 28; BaLL LunLa 62; Belka10 80; bergamont 84; Beto Chagas 69; Binh Thanh Bui 84; Bloomicon 54; BlueSkyImage 69; Bo1982 77; Bohbeh 46; bonchan *covers*, 76; BOONCHUAY PROMJIAM 67; bright 24; Butterfly Hunter 16; Busurmanov 32; Bychykhin Olexandr 44; Byron Ortiz 82; byvalet 72; Caftor 23; Catwalk Photos 75; CHAjAMP 20, 39; ChameleonsEye 32; chanut iamnoy 25; charnsitr 39; Chinaview *covers*, 60; Chones 80; Chuanthit Kunlayanamitre 82; Chubarov Alexandr 32; Chutima Chaochaiya 48; Coffeemill 66; Coprid 43; cowardlion 30; Creativa Images 12, 21; Csdesign86 38; Dacian G 54; Dario Sabljak 60; Dark Moon Pictures 36; Dashu Xinganling 46; Dean Drobot 71; defpicture 66; demidoff 37; Denis Rozhnovsky 54; DenisNata 2, 15; Det-anan 14; Dimasik_sh 15; DK Arts 60; Dmitriy Bryndin 74; dotshock 19, 69; Dragan Milovanovic 28; Dragon Images 13, 21, 46, 53, 58, 62, 68; dugdax 65; DVARG 54; East 20; Ebtikar 34; Ekaterina Pokrovsky *covers*; Ekkamai Chaikanta 80; Elena Elisseeva 80; Elena Schweitzer 82; Elena Vasilchenko 62; Elina-Lava 75; Elnur 24, 28, 74; elwynn 2, 17, 20, 28; Enlightened Media 83; Eric Isselee 25, 66, 67; ESB Professional 23, 35, 37, 48; Eugene Onischenko 68; Evan Lorne 57; Evangelos 32; Evgenyi 85; Fat Jackey 26; fear1ess 57; FeellFree 82; feelplus 35; Ferenc Szelepcsenyi 61; fizkes 64; Flashon Studio 59; focal point 50; fotohunter *covers*, 42; Fototaras 47; Francesco83 18; Frank Fiedler *covers*, 22; Freedom_Studio 35; furtseff 60; gallimaufry *covers*, 67; Geo Martinez 13; George Dolgikh *covers*, 22, 81; Gino Santa Maria *covers*, 50; Gnilenkov Aleksey 37; gogoiso 28; Goodmorning3am 64; GooDween123 36; gowithstock 80; Green Jo 42; Grobler du Preez 67; Guan jiangchi 67; Gumpanat 27; Halfbottle 34, 47; Hallgerd 36; Hans Kim 34, 54; HelloRF Zcool 48; HomeStudio 24; Hong Vo 83; Howard Sandler 75; humphery 57; Hung Chung Chih 72; Hurst Photo 69; hxdbzxy 48; hxdyl 76; I'm friday 32; Iakov Filimonov 27, 34; IB Photography 54; ifong 24, 32; Igor Plotnikov 72; Igors Rusakovs 85; Igor Sh 80; iko 16; imtmphoto 11; inbevel 43; IndigoLT 74; Inna Astakhova 67; interstid *covers*, 10; iofoto 12, 13; irin-k 29, 67; Ivan Demyanov 24; Ivan Smuk 69; Ivan Trizlic 13; Jane0606 57; jaroslava V 66; jazz3311 81; Jeanne McRight 59; jianbing Lee 46; JIANG HONGYAN 84; jiangdi 85; John Bill 43; joyfull *covers*, 30, 33; junpinzon 30, 31, 33; Kamenetskiy Konstantin 10, 11, 68; Karkas 37; Karramba Production 69; Kate Aedon 21; Kaveex 64; kazoka 43; Kazuki Nakagawa 36; kedrov 28; Keith Homan 80; Khomulo Anna 70; Kim JinKwon 75; Kirill Vorobyev 67; kirillov alexey 72; Kletr 67; Kobby Dagan *covers*; Kongsak 76; Konstantin Aksenov 70; Konstantin Zubarev 28, 29; KPG Ivary 39; KPG_Payless 36, 76; Ksander 54; kudla 70; Kzenon *covers*, 25, 31, 45; LazyFocus 67; Lemberg Vector studio 56; leolintang 75; Leonid Ikan 42; leungchopan 2, 10, 13, 57, 58, 59, 70; Lev Kropotov 65; LifetimeStock 74; Lim Yong Hian 82; Linda Bucklin 66; Lisa-Lisa 32; livingpitty 39; Ljupco Smokovski 65; Lonely 36; Lotus Images 45; LuckyImages 59; Lunghammer 68; M.Stasy 46; Macrovector 15; Madlen 83; Makistock 2, 58; Maks Narodenko 82; Marcos Mesa Sam Wordley 23; Maridav 42, 69; Mark Cha 39; maroke 59; martinho Smart 14; Matej Kastelic 70; mathom 24; Maxim Tupikov 69; maximmmmum 44; Maxx-Studio 70; michaeljung 53; 70, 74; MidoSemsem 82; Milles Studio 45; Ministr-84 32; mirana 55; miya227 10, 27; Monkey Business Images 11, 12, 14, 46, 58; monticello 79; mountainpix 75; mphot 61; MSSA 17; MuchMania 72; Myibean 82; Nadya Chetah 44; Nagy-Bagoly Arpad 61; naka-stockphoto 11; Natalia D. 67; Natalya Aksenova 67; Nawanon 68; Nerthuz 33, 64; Nghia Khanh 72; nik7ch 14; Nikita Rogul 31; Nikki Zalewski 22; Nikolas_jkd 38; Ninja SS *covers*; NIPAPORN PANYACHAROEN 85; Normand Fernandez 31; ntstudio 82; nui7711 57; number-one 21, 74; NYS 28; oatawa 39; odd-add 42; Odua Images 13, 39, 40, 76; Oksana Mizina 83; oksana2010 67; Olesia Bilkei 37; Ollinka 37; onair 82; Orgus88 44; ostill 64, 69; OZaiachin 60; Palis Michalis 54; panda3800 *covers*, 82; Paolo Bona 68; pathdoc 34; Patrick Krabeepetcharat 76; paulaphoto 12; pcruciatti 56; Pepsco Studio 56; Periplus Editions (HK) Ltd. 49; Peter Hermes Furian 72; Petronilo G. Dangoy Jr. 44; Phattana Stock 58; photka 47; photo5963_shutter 25; Photographee.eu 15; photomaster 67; photosync 67; Phovoir 74; Phuong D. Nguyen 33; Picsfive 80, 82; pio3 69; pisaphotography 72; Piti Tan 77; pixelheadphoto digitalskillet *covers*, 13; Pixel Embargo 27; PORTRAIT IMAGES ASIA BY NONWARIT 20; PR Image Factory 15; Praisaeng 75; Prasit Rodphan 48; Pressmaster 44, 68; Preto Perola 46; PrinceOfLove 58, 80; ProfStocker 43; pryzmat 27; Puripat Lertpunyaroj *covers*; Quality Stock Arts 57; qvist 26; Rachata Teyparsit 13; racorn 48; RAGMA IMAGES 13; rangizzz 82; ratmaner 37; Rawpixel.com 32, 65, 70, 76; Rido 76; risteski goce 33; Rob Wilson 30; Romaset 62; RossHelen 28; RTimages 38; Rudchenko Liliia 84; Ruslan Merzliakov 85; Ryszard Stelmachowicz 37; S-F 67; saiko3p 82; Santibhavank P 62; Scanrail1 80; Scanrail1 46; ScriptX 79; Sean Locke Photography 40; sezer66 65; Shamaan 39; Shanti Hesse 70; Sharaf Maksumov 57; shopplaywood 34; Shumo4ka 22; Sinseeho 16; skyfish 42; Smileus 42; sociologas 22; Solomatina Julia 22; solomon7 56; SOMMAI 84; Son Hoang Tran 61; Sonya illustration 22; Spacedromedary 27; spiber. de 46; potmatik Ltd 62; ssuaphotos 84; Stanisic Vladimir 56; Stanislav Khokholkov 74; Starikov Pavel 57; steamroller_blues 81; Stephen Coburn 53; stockphoto mania 30; stockphoto-graf 81; Stone36 37; Stuart Jenner 3, 10, 21, 58, 82; studioloco 43; suvita style 13; Syda Productions 70; Sylvie Bouchard 56; szefei 46, 68, 75; takayuki 12, 21; tanuha2001 56, 80; Tappasan Phurisamrit *covers*; taveesak srisomthavil 42; TB studio 77; Teguh Mujiono 17; TENGLAO 75; The Len 43; themorningglory 70; Tim UR 83; timquo 51, 83; Tobik 84; Tom Wang 3, 10, 16, 36, 44, 46, 49, 64; Tony Magdaraog 75; topseller 45; TRINACRIA PHOTO 47; Tropper2000 82; TTstudio 65; Tupungato 30; ucchie79 13; Valdis Skudre 36; Valentyn Volkov 82; vandycan *covers*, 29; vectorshape 55; Veronica Louro 32; vhpfoto 36; Viktar Malyshchyts 82; vipman 15; Visaro 31; visivastudio 24; vitals 83; Vitaly Korovin 19; Vlad Teodor 28; Vladimir Wrangel 66; VOJTa Herout 72; Wallenrock 80; waltericricsy 31; wavebreakmedia 24, 58, 61, 68; WDG_Photo 64; Wire_man 32; wissmacky 34; WitthayaP 13; wong sze yuen 44; wong yu liang 2, 59; YanLev 45; Yuganov Konstantin 53; Yuri Samsonov 80; Zacarias Pereira da Mata 37; zcw 81; zeljkodan 45; Zerbor 63; ZeroThree 50; zhu difeng 30; ZinaidaSopina 30; ZQFotography 2, 59; Zush 85

Hindi mahirap matutunan ang wikang Filipino.
Tagalog is not a difficult language to learn.

mga kulay
colors

sumayaw
to dance

kalesa
horse carriage

mga kaibigan
friends

gitara
guitar

lumpia
Filipino spring roll made
with vegetables